THE PRESENT CRISIS

A Survey and Critical Analysis of the Human Mind
As it Exists in Our Time.

D1597620

By
Gopi Krishna

NEW CONCEPTS PUBLISHING, INC.
NEW YORK
1981

ISBN: 0-941136-01-9
LIBRARY OF CONGRESS CATALOG CARD NUMBER 81-83446
COPYRIGHT © 1981 BY GOPI KRISHNA
ALL RIGHTS RESERVED
PRINTED IN THE UNITED STATES OF AMERICA
FIRST EDITION

ACKNOWLEDGEMENTS

COVER ILLUSTRATION: "Christ Crucified." by Francisco de
Zurbaran, is reproduced through the courtesy of The Art Institute
of Chicago. Signed and dated 1627, this life-size oil on canvas was
painted for the Dominican monastery of San Pablo, Spain, and
was immediately recognized as a masterpiece and considered to
be Zurbaran's greatest work. "The Ascension" is from a series of
paintings by Harold Copping, published in 1907 under the title,
Scenes in the Life of Our Lord.
INSIDE ILLUSTRATIONS: These 10 engravings, illustrative of
the Bible, are by the 19th Century genius, Gustave Dore, and
were published in 1883 as part of a collection of 100 in *The Dore
Bible Gallery.*
GLOSSARY: Prepared by G. Philippe Menos and Karen A. Jones.
TYPOGRAPHY: S-O-S Typesetting.
DESIGN AND PRODUCTION: Ronald Bough Studio.

CONTENTS

INTRODUCTION

"Through all the period of writing this work, I was myself overwhelmed with wonder at the way in which I was guided to take down this Message," the author recalls. "I even now feel, after reading it over and over again, that I could never be the author. It is an Intelligence beyond our comprehension from which it has come.

"I could actually feel a Superior Intelligence intervening when ideas, crystalized into words strung in order like a necklace, floated before my inner vision to be put down on paper. The manner in which the most profound problems of human life are discussed with brevity and precision is so amazing, at least for me, that I am lost in wonder when I recall that many of these paragraphs were written down as if I was copying from an invisible open book in front of me."

Now in his seventy-eighth year, Gopi Krishna is the author of more than a dozen books. None, however, is so extraordinary as *The Present Crisis.*

For him, it is a "Wonderbook," radically different from any of his previous writings. "I believe a new chapter has opened in my life and a new phase has begun," he says.

Though the book deals with the present extremely complex and explosive state of the world, it was completed in an incredibly short span of time—less than three weeks. The variety of subjects discussed in the work is amazing. Almost all the aspects of human life are covered, and the most urgent problems of the day are dealt with in a manner which is astonishing.

It discusses freely the reason for the present crisis, the remedies that can be applied to solve it peacefully and the dreadful consequences that might ensue if no attempt is made by the powers concerned to ease the tensions and stop showing each other down, which now upsets the peace and tranquility of the world.

"Mentally, mankind has become fossilized," the author says. "We should not be misled by satellites, spaceships and computers. They are machines and cannot take the place of the human intellect. If the wit of mankind becomes distorted, there is no hope for the race.

"We can see, when we look around, what dust and cobwebs have gathered on our political and social systems, on our religion and in the way in which mankind, even at this elevated state of her existence, spends her life."

The Present Crisis is aimed to clean away these

cobwebs and this dust and make the race look at herself in a mirror, which can reflect her visage in such a clear way that the mistakes and the errors become clearly perceptible, the author says.

"We cannot see them, as we have become inured to them, and both our conscience and our wit refuse to show us the ugly reality. The race cannot survive during the nuclear age unless there occurs a complete change in our social and political structures, and spirituality, pruned of all superstition and falsehood, becomes the guiding star of our life."

Unlike any prose or verse he has written so far, this book has several characteristics which never appeared in his works before. It is ironical, satirical, biting, comical and humorous at the same time.

Some of the topics, as for instance the current theory of evolution, psychic research, the present hectic race for wealth and possession, have been dealt with in a way which never could have been accomplished in the author's normal diction.

The main object of *The Present Crisis,* he believes, is to prove that Inspiration and Revelation are verifiable phenomena which need the urgent attention of the leading scholars and scientists. It is the investigation of these phenomena, he says, that will put science on the track of real religious experience, which has been at the base of every faith existing at present.

PREFACE

This book shall not be sent for press reviews,
Discolored often by reviewers' whims,
Nor cater to the needs of publishers,
More keen on sales than merits of a work,
Nor flatter wearers of imperial crowns,
Who fail to strive for a united race,
Nor pander to the self-indulgent rich,
Lax in providing earth with lasting peace,
Nor pamper those self-righteous holymen,
Who thirst more for disciples than for God,
Nor honor egotistic scholars who,
In this grave crisis, fail to serve mankind,
Nor humor passing readers hungry for
Thrill and adventure in the stuff they read.

But it shall come straight before the eyes
Of simple, honest folk of every land,
Unvarnished, with no comments or remarks
From high-flown commentators who themselves
Benighted, make the rest, too, lose their way.
The appeal it makes is first addressed to those
Who feel like strangers in this giddy world,
Devoted more to flashy splendor than
Unceasing search for truth and lasting good,
Whose open, loyal hearts rebel against
The double norms and standards of our time,
Against injustice, sham, deception, fraud,
Masquerading as truths and principles,
As clear to honest eyes as mid-day sun,
And who devoutly pray for healthy change
So that all live in friendship, peace and joy,
True to humanity, themselves and God.

April 13, 1981.

Gopi Krishna

LIST OF ILLUSTRATIONS

THE TOWER OF BABEL
Genesis xi.

Having all one language, now nothing was restrained from them which they imagined to do. So the Lord did there confound their Language and from thence scatter them abroad upon the face of all the earth.

CHAPTER I

THE MAJOR CAUSE
OF ALL TURMOIL

The object of this writing is to paint
The world as it is, not as we believe
It to be, nor as we glean from the books
Or every day learn from the media,
Nor as our vested interests dictate,
Nor as we choose to see it in the light
Of our profession, avocation, trade,
Position, office, color, creed or caste,
Which blur our honest vision of the world;
And make us so oblivious to those things
Essential for our welfare and our growth,
That we must change our attitude and try
To be much more objective in our views.
'Tis time now for this reappraisal to
Prevent an oncoming calamity.

A hundred thousand books with varied views,
As many papers with conflicting news,

As many scholars, writers, editors
And speakers o'er the other media
Inject their thought into the passive brain
Of human beings ruthlessly to bring
Them round to their own way of seeing things,
Not for instructing them in what is right,
Nor for reporting honestly the news,
Nor making them aware of what is what;
But for the purpose of a roaring trade:
The veiling and distortion of the truth!

This faulty habit of our century,
To expose the extremely tender human brain
To endless volleys of commercial thought,
Delivered mindless of its soundness, truth,
Integrity or worth, for ready cash,
Must be reformed before it is too late.

Can you believe it that the major cause
For all unrest and turmoil in this age
Is that the highest talent and best pen
Are oft on sale and can be bought or sold
By men in power, by traders and the rich,
To throw dust into the eyes of the crowds,
To make them see what they like them to see,
To make them think as they wish them to think,
And act as they, at heart, want them to act.

Perhaps you are astonished at the hint,
But mind of all our thinking is the mint.

How can unbiased thought come out of it,
When it depends on someone for its bread;
When, in these times, with such a battle on
For mere subsistence, intellect becomes
Subservient to one who buys her up,
Who takes care of her shelter, clothes and bread,
And thus acquires a hold upon her which
She cannot shake off and must put up with,
Howe'er distasteful this control might be?
Crowds of dependant intellects abhor
Their masters and their own positions, too.

The greatest error of our day is that
We have reduced the richest products of
Our culture to the station of a serf,
To kneel before the rich and powerful;
And use their pen as they bid them to do,
Support what they approve, rebut what they
Dislike, thus making our supreme ideals
Not talent, truth or right, but power and gold;
Material objects which, condemned by faith,
Hold e'en the God-fearing in their grip,
Because they know not that religion came
To save evolving man from this mistake.

In this discussion pray keep it in mind,
There are good men in every walk of life,
Conscientious, noble, truthful and sincere,
Who try to do their duties honestly,
To the best of their lights, so that no harm

Is done, no error made in what they do,
With the approval of their conscience and
Their God, in the discharge of duties owed
To their employers, families and friends,
And all those with whom they are somehow linked
Or have a place in their lives in some way.

This honest class, which forms the healthy core
Of all societies, groups, nations, crowds,
Professions, occupations, hobbies, trades,
Of clergy, seekers after God or those
Who take to mediumship or sorcery,
Is much out-numbered in this hectic age
By those who throw all principles to winds
To serve their ends — a state of malaise which,
If cured not, acts like cancer on a folk,
Who lack the impulse e'en to heal themselves,
And turns them into a swollen, putrid mass,
That grows more proud the more it sinks in mud.
Without this solid core of men and dames,
The hollow bulk of mankind would be lost.

In our allusions to the faulty gents,
Who are responsible for the grievous harm,
Done by them to the race in mad pursuit
Of base objectives and unworthy aims,
Or their ambitious plans and selfish ends,
The criticism is aimed at only those
Who overstep the bound of principles
Of truth, integrity and honesty,

Impose upon the people or betray
Their trust to win success for their own plans.

This gentry is in every walk of life,
In business, politics, professions, trades,
Among the scholars, priests, the rich and poor;
Or psychics, yogis, ascetics and saints,
Tycoons, the heads of states and ministers,
Among the worldly and the holy both;
That, more or less, designedly plays a part
In adding to the already heavy load
Of wrong, now slowly edging mankind on
Towards a purifactory ordeal,
Which will be no respecter of one's creed
Or color or class in the gruelling trials.

No one need be offended at the thought
That his or her profession, trade or craft
Is made the object of derision, fun
Or biting criticism or mockery.
There is no aim to injure or offend,
But only to expose the fallacies,
Effete ideas, notions, false beliefs,
Not noticed by their owners of their own,
Which need exposure in a striking way
To bring the error home to those concerned.
In short, the object is to expose the lies,
The shams, impostures, frauds and trickeries,
Of which, at this time, mankind must be pruned
To brave the storm now brewing on the verge.

A storm, born of the fatal weakness in
The mind of man to treat the goods of earth
With far more care than his own precious soul:
To find destruction and extinction more
Acceptable than simple, healthy ways
Of life; to woo death and take it as bride,
Rather than give up prejudice and pride;
To dig the grave of stricken progeny
Rather than call a halt to vanity;
To brave it all for prestige, power or rank,
Until dismembered, broken, blind and lame
Ten million victims of the war would crawl
And hop to beg for alms, as happened in
The world war two to once-proud Germany.

It is incredible how the brilliant minds
Of all the countries, as if laid with rust,
Can put up with the lame excuses made,
Or trust the explanations offered that
This horrid race for more atomic ware
Is run to stop the other side from war,
By using the threat of superior force
To act as a deterrent for the foe.
Time after time the same outdated plea
Is dinned into the ears of anxious folk,
To soften anger or allay their fear,
While arms and ammunition grow apace.

Right from the time when this profane device
Was used in Japan, the infernal plot

Has e'er been wrapped in mystery profound.
It ne'er has seen the light of day, except
For fragments which here or there somehow leaked.
The world in general is still in the dark
That mankind can be ended in a day,
And the earth made a desert overnight.
The masses e'en in the most forward lands
Have but a hazy notion of this threat,
And in the poorer countries, O my God,
Except a few, the bulk knows not a jot.

So these infernal engines grow apace,
While three-fourths of mankind is wrapt in sleep,
Has no idea 'tis so near to death,
No notion that a most malignant plague,
That can devour the whole race, may break out
On any day to swallow every one;
Or that a hundred million thunderbolts
May strike at crowded spots to smash to bits
Millions of homes with all the folk inside.

They know not, O ye brave upholders of
The Right of Man, that there is such a thing
As nuclear missile which can kill at once
A million people and destroy a town.
And 'tis these innocents, Almighty God,
Who will be murdered with the nuclear bolts.

There are now countless groups of earnest souls
Intensely occupied with this one task:

How to prevent the deepening crisis from
Resulting in a nuclear holocaust;
How to create a daily mounting tide
Of protests from peace lovers of all lands
To press the men in power and ruling heads
Of superpowers to ban atomic arms.

There is no task so urgent as this one,
When looked at from a prudent point of view.
For what can all our sweating toil avail,
What good can come out of all we have done
For centuries to make the earth a Heaven,
Of joy and beauty, filled with every need
And lavish luxury, of every kind,
When but a few hours of atomic fire
Can ruthlessly reduce it all to ash?

'Tis unbelievable how with this threat
Of death, now staring in the face of all—
A death so horrible that it defies
All efforts to portray its agonies—
The world should go on with its daily chores,
With its amusements and its pleasantries,
As if there is nothing wrong anywhere,
And all is okay on the Western front!
Nothing to fret about, no one to fear,
All nice and smooth, the nation safe and sound:
A most unhealthy and unnatural frame
Of mind in such a serious crisis which
Can be the grim beginning of the end;

The one cause of extinction of the race;
Of suffering, grief, privation, loss and pain
No skill can paint, no language can describe!
This is the blooming spring of talent, wit
And art, the apex of our knowledge of
The world, the zenith of inventive skill;
The peak of luxury, abundance, wealth,
The heyday of enjoyment, orgies, thrills,
In short, the prime of pleasure-loving lives.

Why in this happy Eden should arise
A Monster, born of flowering science, to hang,
Like to a fearsome specter o'er the earth,
And cause acute suspense, distress and fear
To those who know what evil it portends?
Why in this glamorous age, with minds distraught,
Should we be made to watch the give and take
Of two predominant nations angling for
Support from other people of the earth,
To fight a bloody duel in which none
Will be victorious, none sustain defeat,
None will survive the war unto the end,
And neither ever know who won or lost.

This book records a commentary, in
A higher plane of pure Intelligence,
On how the present world appears, when seen
Divested of the gaudy coat of paint,
Applied by man's inherent urge for show
To hide his frailties from the searching eye

Of his immortal Soul to trick himself
Into believing what he does is right.

This state of Grace, attained by the devout,
Who consecrate themselves, both heart and soul,
To the eternal Quest of probing deep
The awesome mystery of Life and Death,
Permits the surface mind at intervals
To peer behind the heaving Sea of Life,
At the stupendous Ocean out of which
The soul emerges, like a bubble, for
A while, to laugh and grieve upon the stage
Of earth, till it throws off the mortal coil,
No more to be seen in the abandoned dress,
No more to love or be loved in the flesh,
To taste its ecstasies and agonies,
Lost in the vastness of the Ocean of
Terrestrial Consciousness, the Source of Life
On earth, but a drop in the Cosmic Main.

Since the life and survival of the race
Are now at stake, so this appeal is made
To draw the attention of the elect, in power,
Whose word can count in the attempts at peace
Made by pacific groups all o'er the earth,
Which might, if they succeed, avert in time
The dread calamity now staring in
The face of sick mankind.

                              This Message through
A mortal brain, in earthly language, though
In some ways lacking in fidelity,
Has still enough of substance to prove that
Man has subsidiary channels for
Communication with the Cosmic Mind.
The sign is: This inspired prophetic rhyme,
In form, cannot be duplicated by
A normal brain, howe'er accomplished in
The art of poesy, howe'er informed
In knowledge of the world, however skilled
In writing fast on such a complex theme.
Let them who disbelieve this try their best.

How far the candid observations made
In this unplanned, fast-written work, are true
Impartial Time, in due course, shall unfold.
Till then the hasty judgments passed by all
And sundry will in torrents pour to stand
As evidence to prove the fallacy
Of man's dependance on his wit alone,
Ignoring God and intuition, for
The climax of the bloody Drama that
Will be enacted soon shall not conform
To the conjectures of the learned nor
The expectations of the world's elect,
Nor estimates of specialists in war;
Nor to the guesses made by common crowds,
But end up with a Tableau of its own.

THE PHARISEE AND PUBLICAN

Luke xviii.

Humility in contrast with pride or loftiness of heart is a theme strongly
dwelt on in the Bible. That God is with the lowly in spirit is one of the
loftiest as well as tenderest of sacred teachings. Here the self-satisfied
Pharisee praises himself before God, while the self-humiliated Publican,
falling to his knees, confesses his sins.

CHAPTER II

TOWARDS AN
ABERRATED INTELLECT

In this dispassionate survey the first
To come should be the holy men who claim
First-hand experience of the exalted state
Of Samadhi or mystic vision or
Ecstatic trance, Sahaja or Satori,
To mention a few names applied to that
Rich state of consciousness in which the seer
Perceives himself immersed deep in a vast,
Unbounded Ocean of pure Being, lost
In contemplation of a wondrous plane
Of Gnosis, where the sense-bound soul, released
From carnal chains, observes its Unity
With an unnamable Living Presence which
Defies description — one Omniscient
Intelligence, eternal, infinite,
Encompassing the whole creation, yet
Despite its Majesty, the humble self
Of the enravished seer in the trance:

A rare phenomenon which e'er evoked
The keenest interest amongst the wise
From the dim dawn of culture and now forms
The springhead of all revealed religious lore
Of earth, with crystallized directions for
The guidance of the evolving human race.

Apart from this distinguished class, there are
Those who profess some knowledge of this state;
Instruct their disciples in methods, claimed
To be unfailing, which result, they say,
In instant bloom of those rare faculties
That bring about the union of the soul
With the Divine, and grant perennial peace.
Most of them form hot subjects of debate,
Some for and some against the claims put forth,
Some neutral, sitting on the fence to watch,
And some dismissing the whole topic as
Delusion, far beneath their dignity.

But no distinguished scholar has explained
Why, like an epidemic, has this craze
For Yoga, Tantra, Meditation, Zen
Now gripped the minds of millions on the earth.
Why have the attempts made by the elite among
The learned in the last two centuries,
To drive out Faith and occupy the front,
Resulted in this sad debacle and,
Instead of losing, how she has survived
And with redoubled force is back again?

A still-ignored phenomenon so clear
That 'tis surprising none attempts a probe,
For it explains the crises facing Man.

There is another class, distinguished from
The other two, which e'er confines itself
To magic, sorcery, occultism or
Enchantment, witchcraft and the methods used
To gain control of demons, spirits, ghosts
Or astral forces and such entities.
They all deserve a serious study for
They, too, encouraged by the rising tide
Of growing interest in the bizarre,
Have launched a massive drive, but from behind
Their hide-outs, with exciting stories told
Of Yogis, Lamas, Wizards, Masters or
Magicians, Sorcerers and all the rest,
From Tibet, Egypt, Brazil, China or
Himalayan heights and other far off sites,
All very hard to reach.

                              But both the cast
And authors of the dramas e'er remain
Out of sight of the readers, dying now
To catch a sight of them to warm their hearts,
That such incredible beings live on earth;
But neither those in hide-outs nor the cast
Come out in broad daylight to show themselves,
And, like sun-hating bats, keep in the dark,
Leaving the fans in nagging doubt for life.

But, we must not allow this dismal tale,
Or e'en the controversy, raging round
The second class, to blind our vision to
What wonders can be done, if both of them
Join hands with scientists to mend the world,
Which stands in desperate need of such help
To rescue mankind from a mortal threat.
They, too, are helpful as they keep alive
The magic lamp alight in human hearts,
That clay alone is not the only base
Of man's existence or that of the world,
And there exist unbodied entities
And forces for man to explore and scan.

There might be wrong ideas and wrong beliefs
About these planes, but these can be set right
With patient planning, study and research,
And it is for this purpose that we write
To clear the clouds of doubt about the Soul
And put the world upon the trail that may,
In course of time, sift the grain from the chaff.

When did the earth produce a prodigy
In magic, with such skill in spells and charms
Or mastery of astral forces that
He was acclaimed a genius and, as proof
Of his unique, uncanny talents, left
A lasting monument for all to see,
Which still excites the wonder of the world?
Or, when did there arise a man so great

Who made Hermetic Arts an honored science;
Explained the secret of its wonders and
Caused such a stir among the learned that
He ranks now with the most illustrious names
Of earth for his vast knowledge of this lore?

Who e'er included witchcraft, spells and charms
In any category of useful arts?
Not so the illumined, often of the view
That thirst for magic fills a wanton mind,
Which fails to learn from long experience
That it lives in a strictly causal world.
The notion that discarnate forces can
Affect temporal sides of human life,
And set aside the cosmic laws to make
Exceptions in the case of dabblers skilled
In magic, sorcery or kindred arts,
Is but a widely sought chimera which,
No more substantial than a misty ghost,
Melts into thin air at the merest touch
Of hand made to try its solidity.

The hoary sages who, by Grace Divine,
Bequeathed to mankind that immortal thought
Which first revealed to man his destined Path,
In ancient India, ne'er expressed the view
That sorcery is something worth the price
One has to pay to appease the Evil One.
How can they who run after the occult,
Siddhis, miraculous powers or charismas,

Without reflection, gain that state of being
Of which the outer symbol is the "Om?"

Those who by their example, word and deed,
Brought new bloom to the thinking of mankind,
Wore out their noble minds and mortal frames
In the hard effort to uplift the race;
Who firmly curbed their passions and desires,
Ate once a day and used the coarsest wear,
The sour and bitter of life bore with smiles,
To heal the pain, distress and grief of man;
Who bored through mountains, climbed unscalable peaks
Surveyed the sky, explored the depths of earth,
Effaced the barriers of time and space,
To make the world a better place to live,
Are so above those who make it their goal
To master the accursed Satanic arts,
That no comparison is possible
Between the two — the sacrifice of one,
And other's devilries for selfish ends.

When made aware of their angelic lives
We feel an ardent longing in our hearts
To kiss and kiss again their hallowed feet,
For noble actions done and wisdom taught.
It does not matter if the needs of flesh,
Which Nature for good reasons of her own
Has planted deep in every one of us,
Made them to wander from abstemious Paths.
What is of highest moment to the race

Is their outstanding contributions made
For human weal to give the best they had
To turn the earth into a heaven of joy.
Those who out of base reasons of their own,
Look round to pick up holes, when they are gone,
Only reveal the lowness of a mind
Which burns to stab the undefended dead.

Many sit meditating with the aim
To know the secrets of transcendent realms
And deeply probe into the Mysteries,
A thrilling height of mental power to gain.
To win to such a state of Samadhi,
Where Hind or China can be swiftly reached
By astral flight, where any dainty dish
Or charming maid or other tempting ware,
That can assuage one's carnal thirst, a while,
Is brought by airy spirits at command,
Waiting but for a word to obey again
The faintest sign or meet the slightest wish.

When rationally examined such a power,
Which makes a mockery of Nature's Laws,
Is too fantastic to admit belief,
Nor its existence has been e'er confirmed.
Why then, in e'en the most progressive lands
The thought of supernatural prowess grips
The people to such an absurd degree
It has become a rank obsession for
Millions, including scholars of repute,

More pronc to lend belief to exciting myths
Than to the sober truths of higher life,
More keen to study the bizarre displays
Of mind-perplexing psychic forces than
The rich experience of illumined saints.

Were such not the position, how could then
Castaneda's bizarre, fictitious tales,
Conjured up by his own inventive brain,
With no foundation in reality,
Of loathsome drugs, magicians and their craft
Or their repellant rites of sorcery,
Evoke such admiration and applause
From e'en the learned, whom the noble thought
Expressed in scriptures often leaves unmoved?
This grim beginning of a morbid itch
For power and pleasure by unnatural means,
Evinced by such extensive use of drugs,
Will grow in volume with the lapse of time,
An ugly symptom of inner decay,
One of the reasons for the approaching war
To save the fast-deteriorating brain.

Were this position in accord with Nature,
Adepts would steal her treasures every day,
With mantras, yoga, serpent-power or charms,
Making the earth a haunt of astral thieves
And man a prey to diabolic arts.
Imagine what upheavals would disrupt
The happy kingdom of connubial love,

When wizard-lovers willing from afar
Would fill a lovely wife with loathing for
The adoring husband, slowly forcing her,
With hate instilled in her subconscious mind,
To spurn her mate and mad with longing seek
The kisses of the enchanter-paramour.

Absurd, you cry, it ne'er can go so far!
But then why do you madly seek to gain
Control of astral forces, when you feel
That it is too much to expect of them
To cause disruption in the normal life
Of people, or to change the natural course
Of history or into limelight bring
The towering figure of a psychic giant,
Who, by his stunning super-normal feats,
Can cause such an upheaval on the earth
That would force history to honor him?

Men of this stature would be free to cause
Utter confusion in the Cosmic Order,
To flout the laws that might come in the way
Of their capricious plans to satisfy
Their thirst to drink avidly to the dregs
The cup of sensuous pleasure and to steal
Whatever is of value on the earth,
Without compunction for the evil done.

A sixteen-year-old girl, named Kokila,
Of village Uhara in Gujrat, so

Report the papers, is in custody
For murdering two kids, five years of age,
One a girl whom she strangled and then threw
Into a water tank and other child,
A boy, she killed and cast into a well.
The culprit has confessed the crime and said
An exorcist impelled her to this act
To rid herself of a foul spirit, which
Possessed her, and admitted that she planned
To kill a third one to make up the count
Of three such murders she must do to effect
The cure, as spelled out by the exorcist.

The jurists and the scholars who debate
The pros and cons of such phenomena
Of one's possession by a spirit or
Bizarre affections of a similar kind,
Have but to scan, with care, the news reports
In various parts of India, to assess
How often ghastly murders are done with
The aim to appease a god or goddess, or
To find a treasure or avert ill luck,
Expel a spirit from some madcap or
To cure the barrenness of women who
Intensely long to have a darling child.

What grisly murders are committed in
These mad attempts, it is enough to say
That one who reads the accounts for but one year
Would, if he has a heart, feel sick inside,

With horror and disgust, or simply weep
At his own helplessness to end this curse.
This would enlighten them about the way
Deluded people act, when in the grip
Of foolish superstition, who believe
In the existence of unearthly powers
That can bedabble in the affairs of man
And, when propitiated or appeased,
With bloody ritual, grant the favor sought.

The loony gurus who show them the way
Are more condemnable than the chelas who
Believe in them and pay for their mistake
With life-long servitude to crazy heads,
Who keep them busy in performing rites
Or practices that suck their very blood,
Consume their assets and their time and keep
In such a state of hope, suspense and fear
They ne'er enjoy a moment's peace in life.

A hundred cases could be cited to show
What heinous acts are done by stupid folk
When, in the grip of superstition, they
Stone-blind to reason try to appease a whim,
Or to act on the mandate of a Guru—
A fiend incarnated in human shape.
Parents kill children, husbands slay their wives,
Cutting the throats of victims with their hands,
To sprinkle their blood on some deity
Or pour into a stream to win a boon.

A host of ghastly crimes, so heinous that
They foul the very name of sanity,
Cause loud uproar in India every year,
Defeating all the efforts made to cure
This mad itch for uncanny methods used
To quench the fire of some profane desire.

This itch, now travelling to Western lands,
Bespeaks the point wherefrom a virile stock
Begins to slide towards decadency.
Howe'er accomplished, wealthy, strong or shrewd,
It flounders in a marsh which slowly draws
Its mind towards the weird and the bizarre
In lieu of normal, plain and commonplace;
Towards irrational, unsound and false
In place of what is logical and true;
Towards the unnatural and mythical
In place of what is clear and natural.
A man abducted from the broad highway
Of reason and plain common sense, lured by
The charismatic and the magical,
Becomes so much dependant on the help
Of vagrant agencies than his own skill,
That, losing firm faith in himself he turns
To charlatans and phonies for advice,
Unfit to meet the stress of normal life.

No one can cure the fault save by return
To once-discarded hardy ways of life,
Renouncing luxury, abundance and

The wrong desire to have a larger share
By virtue of one's talent, intellect,
Or any God-bestowed superior gift.
Those who incline towards these weird beliefs
Should know that this denotes a growing slant
Towards an aberrated intellect,
Which sharp in some things is confused in others,
And lets its wishful thought and fancy dreams
Distort its vision of reality.

This bundle of hot passions e'er denies
That peace and happiness to his own soul,
Which are a part of its Divine Estate,
And must be moderated to allow
A glimpse of its sovereignty to That,
Imprisoned in the dark lock-house of clay,
Far from the rich dominion which it rules,
Gaining, sometimes, access to it in dreams,
Divested of its shining royal robes,
Its everlasting empire and command,
In billions of embodied forms of life
Fills all the earth and other countless orbs
In space for weighty reasons of its own.

The Monarch in disguise we call the soul,
Encircled by the ego, passion, lust,
Desire, ambition, greed and other foes,
Tarries upon the earth in mute accord
With Laws Eternal it itself has framed,
Drest as a mortal, ranking high or low,

In utter ignorance of its estate,
That 'tis a Sovereign King in his own Right,
The crowning Glory of the Universe,
Whom in our foolish pride of knowledge we
Ignore or e'en deny, to learn in time
When troubled by repeated pricks from Nature,
We shake ourselves free of the enshrouding lust,
And waking up to our Eternal Life,
Become the world and its Creator both.

LAZARUS AND THE RICH MAN
Luke xvi.

"There was a certain rich man, which was clothed in purple and fine linen, and fared sumptuously every day; and there was a certain beggar named Lazarus, which was laid at his gate, full of sores, and desiring to be fed with crumbs which fell from the rich man's table."

CHAPTER III

PULLING THE STRINGS FOR WAR OR PEACE

A wizard ill-disposed towards someone
Could, from a distance, set his beard on fire,
Or break his neck with an invisible blow
Or whisk away his trousers on the road.
One single Miracle-man could with ease
Defeat the most renowned of strongmen met,
With but one blow of his fist kill a host,
Howe'er strong and supple they might be.
One single man controlling but one sprite
Can bring the most aggressive to his knees,
With one look at the specter make him faint,
Immune both to the bullet and the sword.

Who can defend himself from such a foe,
Be he a head of state or minister;
Protected in the most effective way,
He will be vulnerable to the attack.
Into his private room or sleeping chamber

The bulkless phantom can float in like air,
If it bites off his nose or chops off ears,
How can the guardsmen to his rescue come?
If one, by chance, contrives to reach the room,
He would be shocked and stunned when he perceives
His master writhing in such agony,
His body and his bleeding face convulsed,
But no assailant present anywhere;
And wonder at the nature of the fit
That made his chief use his sword on himself.

O, you discerning friends, reflect on this:
How raw are they who take to these pursuits,
To tame discarnate forces with the aim
To use them for appeasing carnal lusts;
Not caring how the Heavenly Court would view
Their doings, when they err to this extent
As to suppose the Lord must be an ass
To allow such anarchy in His domain.

To whom did pious striving grant such power,
That he could bring the earth, air, ocean, sky,
The people and their rulers to his feet?
Did any God-man of this stature rise?
Only crass ignorance is at the root
Of this confusion in unthinking minds,
That God's own Kingdom is devoid of Law,
And there but chaos and disorder reign.
Were there disruption in the heavenly world,
How are our actions then in such good shape?

How does a hen, in that case, teach her young?
How then is system in our flowing thought?
How could we e'er unearth the Laws of Nature,
Were intellect itself unevenly formed?
How could we sagely map the Cosmic Deep,
If we were born of a lunatic Sire?

Strange that even the learned of our day
Are half-believers in these fairytales,
Express their views as if under opium,
"Yes" from this side of mouth, and "no" from that.

Adepts in the sale of this merchandise
Suspend their breathing, look around for signs,
Produce out of air baskets filled with fruit,
Rings, watches, garments, necklaces of pearls.
The dazzled visitors, on whom bestowed,
Amazed at their good luck, assailed by awe,
Do not, perhaps, reflect in calmer moods,
That they could buy them from the market, too.

Were they conjured up by sheer magic power
They would show some sign of the astral world,
A mark or seal or fabric of a kind
That would confirm they are not of the earth.
But they are of prosaic human make,
Millions available always for a price,
But the recipients pay a hundredfold
In cash and kind and mute submission, of
What they would cost if purchased from a store.

Were psychic gifts or magic real boons,
Why do their owners then need food or drink?
Why do their bodies then submit to age,
To grim mortality and fell disease?
But, like the others, they are prone to die
And fall ill, prone to open wide their mouth
To take their tasty, better-spiced food,
With this unearthly sport, too, once a week.

The value of this rare commodity
Is so high, at this time, the vendors ply
A brisk trade such that e'en if they enwrap
Mere earth in paper covers they will sell
Hundreds of thousand with ease in a month.

One with control won o'er a single imp
Or but brief knowledge of the astral world,
Or holding the insignia of a saint,
Who has discerned the formless other Shore,
Or one with expert skill acquired in yoga,
Or a god-man adept in miracles,
Whose honored name is known all o'er the earth,
Revered by millions of true devotees,
Would do a signal favor to the race
Were he to lay flat on the grieving earth
Those self-conceited patrons of "brute-force,"
Much swollen with the pride of nuclear might,
Who in their heart of hearts now plan a move
To overthrow the hated opponent,
But in this process would disrupt the world,
Ruin themselves and gruelling ordeals face.

But none among the living Masters of
Hermetic Arts, in this grave crisis, would
Move e'en his finger to avert the doom,
Although no subject is more pressing now
Than the prevention of this holocaust.
Since they, too, have their irons in the fire,
They cannot give them up to help the cause,
And as there is no hope of their success,
They would but lose their magic when they fail.

So they will not accept this challenge to
Their skill, achievements, reputation, creed,
And would not turn a hair to vindicate
Their honor or to enhance their fame, because
There is not, e'en in name, a solid core
To all what they profess, not e'en a grain
Of truth in the fantastic stories told
By their protagonists to have the pride
Of their association with a being
Who, by some artifice, is widely known,
Hoping to sparkle with the borrowed fame,
But in this effort misinform the world.

It is no wonder then that those who thirst
For the occult, combining their desire
For limelight, would resort to methods which,
When all is said and done, are no more than
Publicity campaigns to draw big crowds,
Throwing a global net in which are caught
Unwary fish that fail to recognize

The trap laid, sometimes paying for their lapse
With life-long bondage to an adventurer.

For such a Master of the spirit hosts,
Or expert psychic or a sorcerer,
With but a little effort, done at ease,
Resolving of the current crisis is
So trifling a task to accomplish soon,
It is amazing none has thought of it,
And billions monthly are, like water, spent
On national defense by wealthly states
That can afford the drain to fortify
Their country 'gainst a prowling enemy.

When, luckily, there are now shining stars
On the occult horizon, whose exploits
And names are widely known all o'er the earth,
The famous writers on these topics or
The known performers of these matchless feats,
And scores of other living honored names,
Of hermits, yogis, tantriks, lamas, saints
Occultists, psychics, miracle-men or
Those who profess some knowledge of this art,
Of any clime or creed, combinedly or
Alone, if well-disposed toward this task,
Could end the crisis easily for good.

Why should they not rush to the rescue of
The race in such a grave exigency,
To save her ship from floundering on the rocks

Of mutual rivalry, contention, hate
By calling to their aid the astral hosts,
Convivial angels, spirits, goblins or
Beyond the earth unseen intelligences,
Which once bent spoons and forks, through earthly pets,
To cause a split e'en in the ranks of science,
Or all of those who claim a direct link
With Super-earthly Beings, that unseen
Cause clamor and commotion on the earth?

The men who pull the strings for war or peace,
In every state, are ne'er more than a few.
But they have all the power for weal or woe,
For storm or calm or, plainly, life and death,
Of happiness and sorrow o'er the rest;
Of making or unmaking all the laws,
Interpreting them as they choose or e'en
Ignoring them, when that can serve their ends.
In short, they are the hubs round which the mass
Of nations turns to toil and sweat all life,
Submissive, like obedient bees and ants,
To do what they are bid, without demur,
Too often flattered by the specious plea
That they live in a great democracy
And are the masters of their destiny.

An obsolete device to invest with power
A handful, with the still more hackneyed prop
Of public ballot, done in rushing haste,
To entrust our life into the hands of those

Whom, maybe, we have never met before;
And seldom can, when once installed in power,
Where they shine, like the moon, so far away,
That few can reach them to pour out their hearts;
Where they are so allured by dignity
That some refuse to own a human heart;
So puffed up with their own importance that
They ride high on the fleeting clouds, while we,
Below them, plod our weary way on earth,
Looking so small and puny to their eyes.

They hold the highest seats in every land
Upon the bowed heads of submissive hosts,
Always aloof and distant from the rest,
Who weave the mantle they hold on their heads;
And show it as their own to all the world;
Usurping all the credit for themselves;
For how can you divide it, say among
A thousand? So they have made it a point,
That only one should wear it on his head,
To be acclaimed the winner of the prize
Won by a working team conjointly,
With hard, exacting toil and endless care,
And those left out, too, must that one applaud.

This is the reason why when wars are won
They heap most of the glory on a few,
And but a fraction on the millions killed,
A topsy-turvy world that must be soon
Set right to dole out every one his due.

A faulty method held tenaciously
By conservative and regressive minds.
A great step forward o'er dictatorship
And monarchy, but still ill-suited to
The present stature of progressive man,
Which must be soon replaced by saner types
Of human order to abolish war;
The only way for mankind to defeat
The all-destroying weapons of our day.

Since this now-burning topic would require
A volume to discuss in more detail,
'Tis time that we revert to where we left
The thread of our discourse to make it clear
That but a fragment holds, in every land,
The seats of power as ruling heads of states,
Members of parliaments, industrialists,
Commanders, generals, ministers or those
Who sway the fate of masses in some way.

But for occult and astral forces or
The spirit armies, or the agents of
Himalayan Masters, it is children's play,
To act in any place to clutch by throat,
To strike dumb, render blind or maim or kill
Or torture or benumb with chilling fright,
One or more of the most aggressive ones,
Among the top men, who hold in their hands
The fate of countless millions everywhere;
But seldom rise above their own beliefs,

Subconscious urges, prejudice and pride,
With this idea always in their mind,
That all their acts are watched from above.

But a few operations of this kind,
Repeated when there is a threat of war,
Would strike the world so speechless with amaze,
And fill with terror e'en the boldest hearts
Among those vested with power everywhere,
That they would form the topic of the day,
Discussed by people in the marketplace,
In trains, in cars or planes where e'er they meet,
Astonished that they ne'er in all their life
Heard anything like this, while some at heart,
Nursing a grouse, would feel a secret joy.

These most macabre incidents would cause
Such an alarm, such panic and uproar,
So rock the earth and shock the frightened crowds
That e'en the boldest would not dare to come
Forward for seats of power in future years,
Except, perhaps, a few daredevils, who
Would die to grapple with these spectral rogues.

Newspapers, bursting out of narrow grooves,
With striking banners, would announce the news,
The radios follow suit in strident tones,
And TV's squander millions but to buy
The rights to shoot, at site, the ghastly scenes
Of haughty statesmen and imperial heads

Of states, who look so grave and solemn as
They stand erect before the cheering crowds,
When in the grip of these phantasmic brutes,
They, faint with pain and horror, would beseech,
On bended knees, the ghostly visitors,
With sobbing breath and tears, to spare their lives,
On promise, sealed with blood, that they would not
Allow their pride, again, to scatter peace.

The picture is not so unreal as
You may suppose. These grisly scenes occur
To meet the ends of Heavenly Justice, when,
In flesh and blood, we see tormented souls.
This weird, unearthly visitation would
Alter the attitude of all those who,
Either by force or by election, hold
The top positions in the lands they rule.

The mere threat of the astral bullies or
The spirit hooligans or ghosts or jinn
Can serve, if wisely planned and utilized,
A strong deterrent, more effective than
The most expensive nuclear armament,
Which has become the precious darling of
The mortals who have chosen the dread path
Of rising in rebellion 'gainst their Lord.

THE SERMON OF THE MOUNT
Matthew v. vi. vii.

Seeing the multitudes, he went up into a mountain, "and it came to pass when Jesus had ended these sayings, the people were astonished at his doctrine. For he taught them as one having authority, and not as the Scribes."

CHAPTER IV

THE MOST-FORBIDDEN SACRED MYSTERIES

It is said Russia is now deep-absorbed
In raising up clairvoyant units, which
Will help the army to foreknow the moves
Of hostile lands, at battle fronts, to learn
Beforehand all their future strategy.
This would give him a great advantage o'er
The Western powers and render null and void
Their plans and preparations for attacks,
By using this new method of defense,
Inducting a new factor in warfare —
The use of super-earthly forces trained
As secret agents, spies or terrorists,
And dread guerillas, all beloved of those
Who use them now as cats'-paws that have made
By their subversions human life so tense.

The Western powers, one safely can assume,
Cannot allow this challenge to their might
To go unanswered, with the grim result
Of losing in the war, and, it might be,
The same devices will be used by them
To counteract the Russian psychic force.

The data of research, designs and plans,
On either side, will not remain concealed
From astral-eyed occult observers, who
Will dart their psychic arrows and fight with
Invisible weapons on the astral front.

From both the camps there will be hard attempts
To wrest the secrets from the rival side,
And bring a part of the war on the earth
Into the interior of the spirit world,
On psychic battlefields, by masters who,
Absorbed in meditation, sit unmoved,
Observing keenly with their inner eyes
What is transpiring on the various fronts.

Were this to happen and in actual fray
Were the superior prowess in this art,
To emerge as a decisive factor in
The fortunes of the war, it will confirm
Existence of the forces and, in time,
By slow development, make psychic power
The most formidable of weapons used
In war, more powerful e'en than nuclear bombs.

It is thus high time that those most concerned
About the approaching global war and its
Grim specter of a holocaust, which is
A nightmare for unnumbered, anxious souls,
Should think of this new method to end war,
And pool all the occult resources of
The earth, apart from those of Russia and
Its mates, to evolve a global strategy,
In order to defeat it at its game,
Or by the mere threat of superior skill
In forming spirit corps and astral squads,
To cow it down before resort to war.

We have a clear advantage on our side
Of great spiritual and psychic wealth,
And Grace abounding of an honored God,
Appeased with worship, prayer, fast and rites,
Attendance at His temple, church or mosque,
Obeisance to the altar, idol, or
The icon or a book inspired by Him,
Obedience to the church dignitaries,
And homage to all those who have renounced
Their homes, their lusts and passion for His sake.

With all this wealth, manpower and Grace Divine,
With all the great exponents of the science,
Now helping eager crowds to achieve these heights,
We are a hundred times in better trim
To fight a winning war with any foe.
And, hence, 'tis time to make a bold attempt

To gain this end and make it widely known
That all Adepts and Masters should unite,
To launch a joint crusade with all their might,
That has no parallel in history,
To end the menace of war for all time,
To vindicate the power of faith in God,
To make use of, for our temporal weal,
The rich resources of the upper world,
Amazing powers and rich potentials which
Can win for us what science could not reach.

Whate'er resources, funds or talent that
We need for this campaign can be amassed
With little effort from supporters, who
Would like to see mankind immune from war.
The only obstacle that might arise
Is that out of the shining galaxy
Of specialists and experts in this field,
Perhaps none or but few would e'er agree
To show their power or exercise their gifts,
To give a practical shape to this plan
And save the race from a catastrophe.

They will refuse to come, on various grounds,
Some treating it as gross indignity
To be approached for such a purpose, which
Is too profane to suit the sacred height
To which they have ascended, far above
The world and its evanescent affairs.
Perhaps, more than they, their admirers and

Their disciples will mount such an assault
Against the firm supporters of the plan,
That sore rebuffed, they will fall back abashed.
The former would continue, as before,
Sitting, encircled by devoted hearts,
Until the hailstorm would disperse the crowds,
When they would loud condemn the war addicts.

Another reason why it is so hard
To carry out the plan to mobilize
The psychical resources of the earth,
Is that the whole domain is thickly wrapt
In such uncertainty and mystery
That no one can assert with confidence
What is a soul or God or spirit or
A jinni, astral being or a ghost,
To what trans-earthly kingdom they belong,
The nature of the forces they command,
How one can be distinguished from the rest?
Where is the man who with authority
Has dwelt on all these aspects of this quest
And drawn a clear-cut picture of the whole?

If you desire to make a life-long search
In this intriguing province, which set fire
To man's imagination from the time
When his brain first to reasoned thought awoke,
Then it behooves you to think on these points
To have a clear idea about this Quest.
For, so far, it has been a hunting ground

For profit, with some chaste exceptions, for
The shrewd, who scattered wide fantastic tales
Of their adventures in this fabled land,
Counting on the credulity of crowds
To swallow the imaginary feasts.

You laugh at this, my dear incredulous friend,
Treating the idea as a fantasy,
A voyage to the erratic land of dreams,
A wishful story or malicious gibe,
Or an Alladin's lamp beyond belief.
I do agree, it must appear to you
Such a fantastic comment on the world,
Such an extremely poor opinion of
The present-day ideas about the occult,
Possession, miracles or psychic gifts,
Siddhis or magic, sorcery and all
That is included in this fancy store,
Sought for by crowds from immemorial times,
But ne'er accepted as proved by all the learned,
Nor e'er confirmed beyond doubt to this day.

Consider for a moment what can be
The logical conclusion of this mess
About the supernatural and the occult,
The world of spirits, magic, wizardry,
Psychic phenomena, miraculous gifts,
Siddhis, possession, witchcraft and the rest,
Save that there is mishandling and misrule
In God's dominion, Him whom we adore

And worship as the embodiment Supreme
Of Truth and Justice, Law and Order or
Of all those countless perfect attributes,
Ascribed to Him in all the gospels, which
We would belie by our acceptance of
These exhibitions as a formal part
Of His Creation, thus rebutting Faith,
Subjecting it to open ridicule,
And making our own views anomalous, too.

If this host of unruly agencies —
All credited with such uncanny power
They can play hide and seek with Cosmic Laws,
Or mold them into any form desired,
Or turn and twist them round their little finger,
Or kick and cuff, as a child does a cur —
Are a part of creation, how can we,
Who are so firmly bound by rigid laws,
Control their movements or make them obey
Our will and may, in fact, lose in the bout?
But, maybe, at a more opportune time
In future, with much more perfected skill
By more advanced human beings, who,
Far more evolved and more enlightened, would
Unearth the secrets of this awful force,
And use judiciously for noble aims,
For lifting up the race or finding God.

The time is not yet appropriate or ripe
To unveil these phantoms or to win them o'er,

Or for attempts to use them, at this stage,
By seekers, still too prone to carnal lusts
For self-aggrandisement, temporal gain,
Or scientific investigation done
To learn the secret of these forces but
To satisfy one's curiosity,
Or hunger for unlimited power or
The wrong desire to have without hard work
Whate'er one wishes for—a fallacy.
And, hence, those ill-advised attempts now made
Are doomed to failure to save erring folk
From fatal consequences, like a child,
Who playing with fire, badly burns itself.
Do e'en the honest savants, who invite
These forces into their laboratories,
Know that they are experimenting with
But phantoms, spooks, discarnate spirits and
The other supernatural entities,
That act as frontier guards to the Divine,
To fool, deceive, mislead and tantalize
Ambitious mortals who wish to unveil
These most-forbidden sacred mysteries,
Without subduing their profane desires,
Or disciplining their bodies and their minds,
Ere launching this herculean enterprise!

The scientists keen to explore this field
But little realize that what they watch,
While sitting taut in tight-shut, darkened rooms,
Are freakish exhibitions of a force

Of which they cannot make the head or tail,
Erratic and capricious to the core,
As much mysterious now as formerly;
And all that they record with minute care
Is but deception, fun and mockery;
The taunting, jocular behavior of
A force of life, obedient to the Soul,
To be aroused, when we equip ourselves
For entry to the territory Divine.

The crazy movements, now observed by us,
Are meant to make us wise to this that we
Have missed the way, and what we see denotes
The outcome of our own unwise revolt
Against the Maker, in the vain attempt
To wander from the Path ordained for Man.

Apart from the elusive forces, which
We have discussed and found beyond our reach,
At least today, for our all-out crusade
'Gainst unbelievers, we have on our side,
What is much more important—Grace of God.
It is surprising that with all this power
Of Truth and heavenly forces on our side,
We should still waver or feel so unsure,
As if we do not trust the word of God,
That He is always on the side of Right,
And, still uncertain, pile up nuclear arms.
Or, might be, that we are not confident
Of our own actions and our state of faith,

Or have a guilty conscience of our faults,
And, hence, are not sure how He would respond,
Or what might be His august feelings on
Our growing passion for a nuclear bout,
Or what are His sublime designs and plans
About the future of humanity.
Or how He views the conduct of the race,
And how we should behave to win His Grace
To emerge as victors in the approaching fight.

Or, it can be, that in our heart of hearts
We are not certain yet that He exists,
Or what the scriptures say is solid truth;
Or that there is a heavenly Judge who knows
Our thoughts and acts, rewards and punishes them;
Or that He really expects of us
A life of prayer, worship, charity,
Humility, love, truth and piety,
And since, in these days, most of us are lax,
We are not so sure how He would react,
Whether He would be gracious to our side,
Keep neutral or side with the hated foe.

Or, can be, we have ne'er thought over this
In depth before, relying on what we learn
From parents or from books or hearsay and
Have never deeply pondered o'er these points.
And, hence, we only have a faint idea
About our faith and God and what that means,
Or may have but a vague, amorphous mass

Of notions and ideas on this theme,
But have not in a systematic way
Thought on it logically to the end,
To clarify the issues of our faith.

This, too, is true that many folk shirk from
The task of putting in good shape their store
Of sacred thought, and e'en slur over gaps,
Without detecting them, in their desire
To appear as knowledgeable to their friends.
Since they have no idea of what they lack,
Nor have sufficient time for study deep,
Nor for discussion with a friend who is
More knowledgeable than they, the void remains;
And save a covering coat of waterpaint,
Which can be rubbed off, the religious mind
Of this type and, perhaps, the major part
Of the devout of any clime or creed
Of our day, are deplorably in lack
Of grounding in the rudiments of faith.

It can be, also, that full many folk
Believe in God, but not that He can be
Involved in mortals' everyday affairs.
They argue that He created us, no doubt,
And is our Maker and that of the world,
The One Primordial Source of all there is;
But how can He be e'er concerned with what
We mortals think or do to live on earth,
And why should He ordain that they must look

To Him for help to set right their concerns?
All that He can expect of vassals is
His worship and remembrance, laud and praise,
Attendance at the church to burn the lights,
To kneel and pray, perform the sacred rites,
Or do what is enjoined by one's faith,
To what-so-e'er religion one belongs.

If we admit that Lord God has no hand
In our affairs, these questions then arise:
Who does then run the Cosmos, who controls
The infinite activity of the Whole?
Who keeps the countless hosts in order, and
Who functions as the Judge Supreme of all,
Dispenses justice, punishes and rewards
And exercises the other powers, ascribed
To Him by almost every faith on earth?

If our acts are to be adjudged by God,
How can we say He has no direct hand
In what we think or do or organize
As persons, groups or nations as a whole?
Those who believe there does exist a God,
How then can they refuse to obey His Laws?
How can they e'er escape the feeling that
All-seeing eyes are always scanning what
They think or do or leave undone to serve
Their selfish interest without a thought
Towards the solemn teachings of their creed?

There are unnumbered men and women whose
Belief in faith and God does not proceed
Beyond their skin, and never penetrates
To thought or act—a most intriguing class
Of people who, when they attend the church
Or talk of God or read the scriptures are
So moved a rain of tears pours from their eyes.

But, when engrossed deep in their worldly strife,
Behave as if there is no God at all,
Extract the utmost pleasure from their lives,
Rebut the teachings of faith by their acts;
Refuse the least concession in their deals;
The least compassion and less charity
Towards the oppressed, the fallen and the poor.
Devoid of fellow feeling they deny
An equal right to any, save themselves,
While reaffirming always their belief
In God and their sincere concern for faith.

Can we suppose an endless series of
Exactly matching, happy accidents
Or countless turns of luck or strokes of chance
Occurred, time after time, without a break,
For astronomical spans of time to make
The earth so well-adapted for the birth
And growth of life, in countless varied forms?
And all the host of meet preliminaries,
Or Ocean of advance designs and plans,
Beyond the power of mortal brains to count,

Came to completion by itself, without
Precise directions from a plumbless Source
Of infinite Intelligence, so vast
That, staggered by Its stark immensity,
Perfidious intellect prefers to avoid
The labor by investing in its place
Insentient matter with unlimited power
Of "Chance" to act as Wisdom absolute:
An odd perversion that must be reversed
To solve the riddle of organic life.

No bright intelligence can be so crude
That she would substitute mechanic whirls
Of lifeless energy to explain a chain
Of orderly events and incidents,
That led to the advent of life on earth.
Only a Providence beyond the grasp
Of human wit could have achieved what was
A miracle, in which a million parts
Had all to be assembled perfectly,
Without a flaw, to make the complex whole
That served as seedbed of terrestrial life.
And 'tis precisely for this reason that
Impetuous scholars often fail to grasp
The magnitude of the Intelligence—
A measureless Deep in which one is lost—
That only can provide the single right
Solution to the most perplexing, still
Unanswered Riddle of the Universe.
Despite the orderliness and the rule

Of Law from atom to the mighty sun,
Like insects which fare best in frigid soil,
They choose the chill of dead universe
To the warm presence of a living God.

When brooding o'er the mystery of life,
To know how it was born and bred on earth,
To find an answer to the questions which
Arise to harass doubt-tormented souls,
With mind unprejudiced and undisturbed,
With passion calmed, desire controlled, and heart
At peace, pray look within and ask yourself
How could it come about haphazardly
That in this raging, storming universe,
A fiery desert of unmeasured size,
There does exist an oasis of peace,
A nursery, protected from the blasts
Of tempests, sweeping o'er sidereal space,
Leaving this tiny niche to bide in calm?

So delicately balanced is this globe,
It is a wonder how it has survived,
With its immense preserves, intact so far;
So varied are the chemical compounds,
Organic and the inorganic both,
That man can never e'en remotely know,
In ages, their count and complexity;
So finely blended is the atmosphere,
That subtlest odors, so extremely faint
A thousand times the olfactory sense

Of man can clearly scent it, as in dogs;
So strongly shielded is frail earthly life
From the bombardment of the cosmic rays,
That if the tough umbrella is removed
A while, all of it would be soon destroyed;
So wisely is environment designed
That e'en the slight pollution caused by man,
Compared to the size of the biosphere,
With his yet maladjusted industry,
For living creatures poses a serious threat.

So well judged is the distance from the sun,
And so well planned the elliptic orbit that
The changing seasons are a boon to life;
So carefully was unarmed man brought up in
The spacious cradle of the Mother earth,
That he survives, while forms, a hundred times
In size, with thickly armored bodies died;
So gently She does her diurnal rounds
That he does not receive the slightest jolt;
So lavishly supplied with all his needs
That he too often over-feeds himself;
So well adorned with beauty for his sake,
That he has picked up all his art from Her;
So bounteous with delicious fruit and grains,
With vegetables, timber, wood and crops,
With lovely flowers, umbrageous trees and plants;
So richly stocked with cattle, horses, sheep,
With cats and dogs, with fishes, beasts and birds,
For company and to fulfill his wants;

So lushly covered with soft carpets of
Luxuriant grasses, spongy turf and herbs;
So finely deckt with rivers, springs and lakes,
With waterfalls, cascades and warbling brooks:
In short, a granary beyond compare,
With hidden treasures still beyond his ken,
So marvellously fashioned and maintained
That mortal intellect reels at the thought:
A rare Elysium for the darling child
For whom the well-concealed maternal love
Of nature has been so exceeding warm
And so solicitous for his welfare that,
Without his knowledge, She has stocked the globe
With all the needs of his predestined rise
To more perceptive states of consciousness.
But, verily, it would be hard to find,
In all the world, a creature so perverse
And thankless as man is, with all his wit,
When he ascribes it all to accident,
Not to the bounty of a gracious God!

With Nature's open book before their eyes
Some scholars, too sure of their intellect,
Find it so hard to reconcile themselves
To their religion, as their vanity
Prevents them from accepting that there is
An Ocean of Intelligence in which
They are but sand grains on the lowest bed.
It is this vanity that blocks the path
To their admission of the patent truth

That man is still evolving, on his way
Towards an un-thought-of superior brain,
To explore the still mysterious world of thought.

It is too much for some to accept this view,
Because it badly hurts their vanity
To think there can be higher minds than theirs,
That see beyond what is perceived by them,
And can disprove their pet ideas and fads,
Which may have brought distinction and renown,
Or are believed sincerely to be true.

This is the reason why religious truths
Are not so palatable to that rank
Of scholars who have high positions in
Materialistic fields, as that would make
Their stand untenable. And since they exceed,
By far, the count of those who honor faith,
The earth's academics refuse to own
The scripture-based idea of man's ascent
To regions of surpassing glory, which
Are far beyond the wildest dream of those
Who proudly flaunt their learning or their rank,
Diplomas or degrees, to establish well
Their right to occupy the front-line seats
In all departments knit with mortal life.

Awareless of the future human Fate,
And of the awesome Wisdom hid behind
The seemingly insentient Nature, lost

In wild conjectures to explain the gaps
In their philosophies which stand unfilled,
They oft commit deplorable mistakes
In their assessment of the Universe,
In the opinions held on Soul and God,
And, as the harvest of this ignorance,
Misguide the race, not knowing where they slip,
Unable to amend the errors made!

EZEKIEL PROPHESYING

Ezekiel ii.

"Thus saith the Lord God. And they, whether they will hear or whether
they will forbear (for they are a rebellious house), yet shall know that
there hath been a Prophet among them."

CHAPTER V

TIME FOR "DARWIN" TO RETIRE

In no book on the subject ever writ,
In no voluminous files of scientists,
Who have been on this study for about
A century now, will you find explained
These points of great importance for the race:
The real nature of the erratic force
Which makes the seance room its sporting ground,
Or of the awakened Center in the brain
Of those who gain the vision of the Self.
This would assuage the thirst of countless hearts
Who ponder o'er the unfathomed mystery
Of their existence, and search for the truth
To know about themselves, the world and God.

I put these questions to the earnest souls,
Who come to me for guidance on this path,
To hundreds of them, but none could explain,
In depth, what he was really thirsty for.

There is no agreement in what they say
About the Soul or God or Cosmos or
The other world or spirits or the occult,
Or spells or magic or the astral plane.
And most of them, except those tutored by
Some one to mold them in his own design,
Their minds, clean as a slate, are much in need
Of right instruction to fill up the void.

There is no agreement because there is
Extreme confusion in the views expressed,
Not only by the scholars and divines
Of yore, but also by the learned of
Our day, who have made the confusion worse
Confounded by their over-zealousness
In taking up the study and research
Of subjects and realms of existence which
Are all beyond the sensual probe of man.
And, hence as e'en a child can understand,
How e'en the most astute of scientists
Or scholars can decide with surety that
The line of study they have taken up
Will lead them anywhere or but confuse
And contradict what they already have learnt
Of the material world and thus create
A gulf between the Seen and the Unseen,
Which is not there, as it can never be
That one part of the cosmos should be ruled
By rigid laws, and other be so loose
That every Tom and Dick can, in this plane,

Do all whate'er he likes to cause a thrill
At his performances to earn his bread,
Or win notoriety so that he is
Embraced and kissed by crowds of charming girls,
Or patted on the shoulders by great men,
Or much sought after by admiring fans
To learn from him the secrets of the trade!

What does he do to cause this loud uproar,
This scramble but to shake him by the hand,
To see in flesh and blood that he exists,
And is not but a myth, to watch his feats
On TV, read in journals or in books,
Or papers that there is a man so great
Who can set nature's stringent laws at naught,
And prove a beneficiary for the race
By demonstrating this rare gift to science?

This matchless being some desire to see
To put the seal of confirmation on
Their own ideas that there do exist
Discarnate forces, which one can control
To break loose from the trammels of the earth.
They feel this way, in their subconscious minds,
Instinctively, but swayed by wrong desire
Or counsel, they translate the impulse so
That it conforms to their own secret wish,
And not to what it should, when rightly grasped,
That their immortal soul, with all these powers
Is waiting to be free of sensory chains.

They wish to watch with their own hungry eyes
Their idol handling these weird forces which,
Call them by whatsoever name you choose,
Delight in causing chaos in all things
And making fools of e'en the erudite
Who, lost in wonder and bewilderment,
Are racking hard their brains to find a sane
And rational solution to these strange
But rare phenomena, accepted by
A massive section of empiricists,
Denied, too, by as large a fragment which
Does not believe the hopeful other half.

But none of them explains this frolic of
A sentient force which, acting through someone,
Consoles, at times, the grief of mourning kith
By bringing greetings from departed kin,
Sometimes unsettles a whole neighborhood
With noise and movement in a haunted house,
Sometimes, assuming spectral shapes and forms,
Excels in wantonness and disregard
Of others' sentiments or property;
Resorts to most erratic ways to show
That it has no respect for man or God,
In short, acts in a way the opposite
Of what religion holds as right and true
For our good in this world and peace in next!

When viewed in this light, those with psychic gifts
Create a schism between man and his Faith.

Save for exciting morbid interest
In weird occurrences no one can explain,
What do they do to merit this applause,
This high degree of interest from the world,
This keen attention from the learned ranks,
And this high honor from the media,
This wide publicity, in the vain hope
That one day these displays would make us wise
About the super-earthly forces, and
Reveal the secrets of miraculous power,
To help man in establishing his sway
O'er the empyrean regions, as he did
On earth—to triumph over both the worlds.

What are the rare achievements they have won?
What are the daring feats they have performed?
What are the exploits that have won them fame?
And what is, after all, the profit gained?
How far has man advanced since this research
Was undertaken by devoted men
And women in face of the hurdles placed
In their way by the angry opponents,
Who were so rigid and unyielding that
It was like striking one's head 'gainst a wall
To try to alter their dogmatic stance,
To let them see the light of reason, free
Of color lent by one's inherent trends,
Which oft determine children's attitude
Towards religion, ere they grow in age,
Mature sufficiently to thrash it out.

This inborn trend in some mistaken minds
Led them to squeeze the whole creation in
The extremely narrow, bony hollow of
The human head, and they delighted in
Their stubborn attitude, denying that
There can be better-fashioned craniums,
On other orbs in space, that can discern
A hundred other subtler planes of life
Which, imperceptible to the normal brain,
Can be discerned with ease by awakened ones.

For such the aim and end of human life
Is concentration on but one pursuit:
How to know more about the physical world,
And use this knowledge to enhance our needs,
To live a lavish and luxurious life,
Where only earth and its resources count,
As they provide us amply with the goods
That make our life a bed of roses for
The flesh, but hot and hectic for the soul,
Raising the problems which we face today—
A view so grievously erroneous that
No blunder made, so far, has caused such harm
To mankind or misled to such extent
The people or created such a rift
Between two sections of the unhappy race,
As this one, which the future shall confirm.

When one begins to enumerate the facts,
While dwelling on this subject, which is still

So vague and nebulous one cannot help
A feeling of frustration, mixed with grief,
And wild desire to laugh at what has been
A decoy to confuse and mystify
The learned, whose approach to this sublime
And solemn Quest was not as reverent
And humble as it should be, in accord
With laws divine, that rule the rise of man
To those heights of perception where he can
Find entry, for the first time, to the planes
To which his own immortal soul belongs;
Planes of surpassing glory, beauty, joy
And all for which we often long in dreams,
All that we find delightful in our art,
In music, painting, poetry and love,
All that makes life worth living for the race,
In short the Fount of beauty, love and bliss
Which, when we climb the dizzy height by steps,
Turns out to be our own immortal soul.

What we ascribe to God in the image which
We frame, eternal life, unbounded joy,
Surpassing glory, majesty and love,
Compassion, mercy, wisdom absolute,
And other holy traits, or those which we
Associate with the ideals framed
Of sweethearts, friends and those of whom we dream,
Or as we greatly wish they should be like,
All these ideals of grace, beauty, charm
And what we attribute to the Divine,

Well up from the deep of our perfect Soul,
The embodiment of all these attributes,
The Ocean from which flows all we conceive
Of God, or His perfection, as the Lord,
Or of the loftiest ideals we form.

That is the reason why religious thought
Has e'er connected with the idea of God,
All that is noble, good and beautiful,
All that is pure, sublime and wonderful,
That is all-knowing and all-powerful,
Benign, compassionate and bountiful;
Because this is the longing of the soul,
The memory of its empire, which it brings
To earth with it when born in human dress,
Exiled from its celestial kingdom for
A while, to be an actor on the stage
Of earth, engrossed deep in the dream of life.

That is why in the temple or the church
Light, music, flowers and fragrance play a part,
Adornments, paintings and images abound,
Why they have oft impressive, grand designs,
Why there is such an atmosphere of peace,
Of solemn silence, awe and calm in them,
Why eerie feelings stir up in a shrine,
In graveyards, in mausoleums and in tombs,
Or in the contemplation of old ruins,
Or ancient monuments, like pyramids,
Because a surge of memories, bursting through
The heavy armor of the surface mind,

When witnessing a grand or solemn scene,
Recalls the soul to its home for a while.

Because intrinsically it is divine,
Majestic, glorious, holy and sublime,
The fount of beauty, symmetry and grace,
Of melody, aesthetics and delight,
Of all that is chivalrous, noble, true,
Harmonious, pure, compassionate and kind,
The cream and essence of the Universe.

That is why in the true ecstatic trance
There stands unveiled a Haven of such peace,
Such grandeur, harmony, perfection, love,
Such glory, majesty and boundless joy,
That one who has the vision is so moved,
And so absorbed, that he forgets the world,
And tears of happiness roll down his cheeks,
Hair stands on end, and his half-open eyes
Reveal the flood of ecstasy and bliss
In which the enraptured soul is wholly drowned.

The mere remembrance of this heaven of joy,
A flash of memory of this paradise,
The briefest recollection of this flight
To the sublime dominion of the soul,
Thrills to the core the ravished human self,
Afloat now on a boundless sea of love,
Eternal beatitude and endless life,
Free of the fear of age, decay and death.

This is a picture of the lofty state
Of mystical experience, Samadhi,
Sahaja, Satori, or rapture or
The state of Union with Divinity.
In spite of variations in detail
The essential features of this rare ascent
To soul's empyrean kingdom are the same.
That is why highest honor has been paid
To those who had the experience anywhere.
Their spoken words and writings were preserved
With utmost love, care and fidelity;
As if instinctively Man is aware
That this Experience is ordained for him.

Under the stress of unhygienic life,
Amid the hot surroundings of today,
This instinct often finds expression in
The wrong desire for super-normal gifts,
Which drives those in whom this perverted urge
Is greater to run after worthies who
Profess some knowledge of hermetic arts,
Like children whose vagarious appetite
Compels them secretly to swallow earth,
In place of dainties offered by their Ma's.

In former times religion held at bay
These ribald wishful dreams of common folk,
This practice of black magic, sorcery,
To gain control of demons, spirits, ghosts
Or other supernatural entities,

Or forces which, it was believed, came from
The Prince of Darkness—the relentless foe
Of man, the greatest hurdle in his way
To God, the Tempter whose anterior aim
Is to obstruct the progress of the soul,
Hold it in bondage with allurements and
Unchaste desires, which pull it down and thus
Prevent salvation and ascent to God.

The cult of magic, white or black, or spells
Or witchcraft, wizardry or sorcery,
Or spirit-raising, charms or similar fads,
Were all condemned as diabolic arts.
Few were the practisers who had the face
In public places to display these wares.
In darkness, secrecy and silence plied
The weird magician his obnoxious trade.
Suspicious at the weirdness of his art,
But also curious, neighbors pried and peeped
To know what devilry was going on.
The simple, guileless folk, though often drawn
To him, yet fear and loath the sorcerer.

But whether simple or intelligent,
The multitude is often strongly drawn
Towards a mystic, saint or anchorite,
A yogi, sadhu or an ascetic,
Not so much for the reason that he has
Control of spirits or miraculous power,

Though this idea, too, lurks in the mind,
But, mainly, that he is austere and pure,
Detached from world and in keen search of God,
Devoid of passion, anger, hatred, greed—
A noble, elevated, kindly soul,
Whose blessings they seek for their welfare or
Upliftment, or prosperity or health,
Instinctively beseeking the same boons
Of worldly good and noble virtues which
Are so essential for the rise of soul.

But uninformed about this Law Divine,
The learned of the age, whose biased minds
Were ill-equipped to pass a verdict on
The riddle of the Origin of Man,
Like Darwin, Monod, and their thinning ranks,
Still in the dark about their very selves,
Their brain, their nervous system, e'en their cells,
Not to say of the driving force of life,
A yet unsolved enigma for the learned;
They cut in hot haste at the tender roots
Of what had been held sacrosanct till then—
The immortal nature of the human soul.

And with this blow demolished the main prop
Of faith, to leave a broken structure for
The church to hold aloft to save it from
The blows of rampant skepticism until
The times improve or Darwin is disproved,
A hope that might materialize now soon.

These ill-advised attacks on Soul and God
Made by impatient, superficial minds,
That are still nescient what their blood contains,
Or how their organs, limbs and muscles work,
Or how bees find their way back to their hives,
But keen to pass premature judgments on
The cosmos and their Maker, rush in haste
Where Wisdom fears to tread and, by this heat,
Commit a grave offense against mankind
By rooting out ideas instilled by faith,
Leaving a blank for charlatans to fill.

It is a riddle how a learned mind,
Which is still floundering in the deep morass
Of scores of major problems that demand
Solution—like the working of the brain—
Should leave them still unsolved to run in haste
To throw a bombshell at the astonished ranks
Of science, leaving them to prove the truth
Of the explosion caused for centuries,
In learned courts, and spend enormous sums
To bear witness in a concocted suit.
The argument that hundreds of astute
And well-known savants, after study deep
And wide research, confirm the theory, taught
All o'er the earth, and treat it as if proved,
Does not take into account the saying old,
That there can be, what happens every day,
A slip between the cup and opened lip.

The time has come for "Darwin" to retire,
Leaving his once redoubtable name among
The authors of exploded myths, who did
Incurable harm to a devout mankind.

The same unhappy fate will overtake
His faulty concept of Heredity
And Natural Selection to account
For man's appearance on once-barren earth.
These two components of his theory are
Deployed as front-guards to defend the base,
To serve as catchwords, never full explained,
And act as brain-traps for a clever mind,
Believing that the problem has been solved,
But not astute enough to grasp the trick
That both the terms designed to untie the knot
Are e'en more knotty than the knot itself.

They give to one the false impression that
The riddle has been answered when, in fact,
It has become more complex than before,
Presenting greater hurdles in the way;
For then the answer was "immortal soul,"
But now we have to grant "heredity"
And "natural selection" and the rest
A greater latitude, creating more
Unanswered riddles than we hope to solve.

Agreed that genes enwomb a wonder-script,
Which stores up knowledge of ancestral traits,

Covering a span of say, a billion years,
Of man's past human and pre-human life.
But who or what decodes this awesome script,
Which by itself provides a clinching proof
That earthly life is not a play of chance,
As, far above the intelligence which found
The code, a billion-times-more-clever wit
Must have devised it for terrestrial life,
To serve for aeons as a fool-proof guide.
Those who refuse to accept the existence of
This superhuman wisdom clear betray
The working of a sealed, unopen mind,
Which rather than believe in what is clear
As crystal, must its utmost try to hunt
For answers to the riddle, which tend more
Towards absurdity than common sense.

Only a quarter-wit can swallow that
The past-belief, amazing genetic code
Can be the slipshod work of fickle chance!
And when was natural selection born
To make it sure the fittest should survive?
Who laid down the criteria how to sift
The fittest from the unfit, the strong from weak?
How then arose the need for sturdy pines,
That live a thousand years, to bow before
The more evolved evanescent butterflies?

It was a most unlucky day for Man,
When scientists in Europe first embraced

The creed of Darwin, that the advent of life
On earth is more explained by calling Chance
To help than by subscribing to the view
That Wisdom absolute ensouls the world!

The puzzle is why should a galaxy
Of brilliant thinkers be on pins to prove
That all this vast creation, known to us,
Is made of only one insentient stuff,
In which Intelligence is out of bounds,
Debarred from entry by the wit of man:
A most outlandish way to look out for
The right solution of a riddle which
Has baffled mankind for ten thousand years;
To be dismissed abruptly as a fib,
Of no importance for the elite of science,
Upon the strength of observations made
By intellects, themselves completely void
Of knowledge how they know and cogitate:
A state of such extreme confusion that
There is no name one can assign to it.
It is, if not exactly, very like
A man observing, through a jaundiced eye,
The yellow color of the objects seen,
Writing book after book to witness that
The Universe is of a citrine hue,
Without subjecting first his own two orbs
Of light to scrutiny to test their sight.

What self-deception and self-mockery;
For if our mind is but a bastard child

Of chance, a whiff from an organic broth,
A freak creation of dead elements,
A wine distilled from pure, fermented earth,
That means it has no province of its own,
No name, no home, address or parentage,
No friend or kinsman in the universe,
A total stranger from no country, who
Just dropped from the clouds on barren earth;
First seen in funny forms, akin to apes,
Before that costume, heaven alone knows what,
But who, all at once, during recent times,
Began to pose as an authority
On how he first appeared upon this globe,
And finally, through some empiricists,
Discovered he was but a bantling, who,
Surprisingly, believes that what he says
About his pedigree, the universe,
And other topics is pure, gospel truth
That must be sworn to as legitimate!

A foundling, who has not the least idea
About himself, presuming to dictate
That his opinions are beyond dispute,
His spoken words denote the final say,
And his conclusions proven to the hilt:
A coxcomb who declares he is but froth,
And yet demands respect for what he says,
Is anxious to usurp the foremost row,
To have the best of dainties and the creams,
Among the learned and the laity both.

Or, might be, what he says is but a ruse
Only to vent his spite against the church,
Or, by perversity, to earn a name!

Ah, what clouding of the intellect
To hold a product of capricious chance,
Who has no mark of authenticity,
No stamp attesting to his genuineness,
No firm position in the Universe,
As worth the slightest credence for the thought
Expressed about the Cosmos and himself.
But, strange to say, this freak is much esteemed,
His counsels listened to, his views imbibed,
His books avidly read, his art admired,
His person, too, is honored and revered
By millions in a famous statesman or
Distinguished scholar, priest, musician,
Discoverer, artist, saint, explorer or
Inventor and in other hundred roles.
Some are impressed so well by his exploits
That they nigh worship him as their ideal,
His picture keep uphanging in their rooms,
Or e'er abiding in their loyal hearts,
At no time do they have the slightest thought
That they bow but to an alchemic toy.

If such is his ill fame, why should he be
Awarded prizes and distinctions for
Unique achievements in some worthy cause,
Regarded with respect, applauded loud,
When he addresses a group or talks to friends?

Why then his works of art or melodies,
His songs, his science and philosophy
Have been preserved for many thousand years?
And why none has the courage e'er to say
That all this treasured store, devoutly kept,
Has for its author but a chance-distilled,
Material stuff, as volatile as scent,
No more substantial than a perfume is.

No one, not e'en the evolutionists
Remind a comrade he is but a hoax,
Who has no substance and no lasting worth,
No seal of office or authority,
A mere excrescence of the mortal frame,
Which grows from it to disappear at death,
A glowworm which believes it is the sun,
A stone mistaken for a diamond;
A wraith impersonating as a prince,
A fleeting breath soon to evaporate,
Without disclosing its identity.
A mere non-entity that has no place
Among the elect—an effervescence pure,
Of which no one has solved the riddle yet,
Nor met it face to face to see it close,
Unseen; as if it is not of the earth,
Like to a bubble which dissolves for e'er
Into the water from which it is born;
Not e'en comparable to a grain of sand,
Which has the hope, at least, of lasting life,
Although it might be scattered by the wind,

But is, as matter, indestructible,
More lasting than the transient human soul!

This is the inglorious depth to which, without
Sufficient proof, some of the learned dons
Of our day have debased the state of Man,
Refusing him the title e'en to claim
The citizenship of the Universe,
To which they e'en to atoms grant the right.
But, as if highly jealous of their kind,
Insist on man's expulsion from the file
Of those included in the honored list
Of their beloved compounds and elements,
Of pebbles, boulders, metals, water, air or fire,
As he is not fit for their company,
For his unstable, vapory character.

They gather every proof and evidence,
Use every plea, pretense and argument,
Their erudition and experience,
Their skillful penmanship and eloquence,
And try their utmost, labor day and night
On massive volumes of jaw-breaking words,
To prove that he is but a breezy puff
Of air, a chemical compound, unknown,
From an experiment which went so wrong
That, in place of a syrup, we have Man.
This is what Monod and his likes assert.

They wish us to believe that earth sustains
Four billion samples of a most unique
Fermented liquor, bottled in the flesh,
Which thinks, imagines, reasons and behaves
As if the earth belongs to it alone,
And held a captive by the enormous globe,
Cut off from other forms of cosmic life,
By far superior to this boastful brand,
Believes it is unmatched in skill and wit;
And with this false conception of itself
Delivers foolish judgments right and left,
On matters far beyond its present grasp,
Oblivious that one rocking tremor of
The earth can end its clatter in no time.

This foaming spirit, when, with knowledge drunk,
Indulges in ill vagaries of thought
Of the sick type we are discussing now;
Evaporating, when the bottle breaks,
To mingle with the void from where it came,
Leaving, at times, a bottleneck behind,
In flagrant theories which when scattered wide,
In tiny bits become embedded in
Precocious brains, to cause the running sores
Now driving Man towards a precipice,
Enticed away from his alloted Path
By some of his own shining intellects,
Among the highest earth has e'er produced,
Lost in the labyrinth of their own wit,
For lack of guidance from the Light Divine.

THE DESTRUCTION OF SENNACHERIB'S HOST
Isaiah xxxvi, xxxvii.

By successive conquests Sennacherib, the mightiest of the Assyrian kings,
extended his dominion over the surrounding nations. But before the last
great battle was to occur, "the Angel of the Lord went forth and smote . . .
a hundred and four score and five thousand; and when they arose in the
morning, behold, they were all dead corpses."

CHAPTER VI

A VINDICATION OF RELIGIOUS TRUTHS

Compare the goal of noble striving for
Unfoldment of the soul, and the ascent
To glorious regions of Eternal Life,
With what the seekers after the occult
Or psychic gifts or magic have in mind,
And mark the yawning gulf between the two.
If one is done to lift the soul to heaven,
The other is to plunge it into hell,
To make this glorious orb of deathless life
A slave to spirits, demons, imps or jinn,
To appease the carnal lusts of aging flesh,
And see their loathsome forms with horror and
Repentance at the awesome time of death.

What have we gained by spending millions on
This study and research for scores of years,
Conducted by devoted pioneers,
Who braved the scorn, contempt and ridicule

Of their compeers and trenchant criticism
From skeptics and the press, but ne'er retraced
The step they took, and bravely plodded on
Till they set moving, with their honest zeal,
A wave of wide approval for their work,
And broader agreement with their results.

The outcome is that in the learned ranks
The opposition is now not so strong,
And more and more of scientists, it seems,
Are coming closer to those who believe
That these phenomena do have a base,
Which further study and research can trace.

Another reason for this change of view,
Among the learned ranks, can also be
Their own frustration stemming from the fact
That science has, up till now, always failed
In finding irrefutable evidence
To prove that it is now beyond dispute
That Darwin, in his theory, has been right
In this: that man rose from the earth by chance.

Not only this they feel more insecure,
For there have crept in other lacunae,
As, holding to their view, they cannot show
That psychical phenomena are false.
So their position is somewhat akin
To one between the devil and deep sea:
They cannot prove their theories nor disprove

What psychical research has brought to light.
It does not matter if a thousand books
Are writ on either side for and against
The views held by the two divided ranks
Of science, and each blames the other for
Imperfect observation, faulty probe,
Defective analyses, or e'en deceit.
But what is crucial for our purpose now
Is that empiricists are split up in
Two schools of thought: One not prepared to own
That there exist intangible forces, which
Can act in ways not covered by the laws
Of matter, known to us, the other as
Assertive in its view that they exist.

What is important in this hot debate
Is not that this one or that side is right,
But that the ship of science is adrift
On Ocean water and none of the crew
Is e'en aware what port they have to make,
Where will the uncharted pleasure voyage end?
For misadventure who will pay the cost?
And who will sound the alarm, when they collide
With super-mundane powers that keep a watch
On fugitives from heaven, to bar the way
And drive them back to where they wandered from
The Path, which smooth or rough they have to tread?

It might be argued how this present split,
Among the ranks of science, can affect

Our fortunes, for the said debate relates
To elements and forces which, in fact,
Have little relevance to human life,
Or to our day-to-day pursuits and tasks?
There might be supernatural forces or
There might not be, they have no bearing on
Our own existence, what we mainly need
Is but a healthy life of honor, wealth,
Abundance, joy, amusement and the rest.
This is what man has always striven for,
This is what he will strive for till the end.

But in this oft repeated answer to
This vital question have you given thought
To this extremely urgent issue, which
Demands our full attention at this time;
Calls for the most effective steps to ease
The mounting tension 'twixt the superpowers;
Requires the full support of everyone,
Among religious-minded friends of peace,
Of every scholar of whatever creed,
For in the coming crisis we are face
To face with the same problem of the past:
Religious fanaticism at its peak,
Grim preparations for a dread crusade
Which might be fought with lethal nuclear arms,
To plunge the earth into infernal gloom,
Reduce mankind to an appalling plight,
And cause a devastation that would leave
Its hideous stamp on earth for centuries.

Perhaps you ne'er have given thought before
To this one aspect of the coming war,
Could ne'er imagine that e'en in this age
Credal fanaticism could gain so firm
A hold on e'en todays' progressive minds,
And pose a problem which none can resolve;
And which, but few of us can rightly grasp!
A serious crisis which is mounting up,
With each addition to the nuclear stock,
Sucking the blood of millions with the drain
On the resources of the states involved.

We ne'er have thought of it that way, because
No one has e'er explained it in that light;
Not one of those on whom we oft depend
For our opinions, notions, thoughts and views —
The statesmen, scholars and the media—
Has e'er touched it e'en with a pair of tongs;
And seem to revel in the attempt to keep
The human world entirely in the dark
About an issue vital for world peace,
About the life and safety of the race!
No, no one has presented this dispute;
This nigh insane dissension 'twixt the two
Most forward nations, each striving for
A signal triumph in the armor race —
Manpower, resources, strategy and skill—
To liquidate the other when desired,
Fanaticism and hatred at their peak.
No one imagines it, because we think

Religious wars are a thing of the past,
And it would be blasphemous to suppose
That skeptic Russia or the liberal West
Would come to blows on such a flimsy ground,
Or pound each other to a bloody pulp,
Simply because they differ in their creeds;
Or for the reason they have diverse faiths.

Read through the bulky volumes of the learned,
Or hear orations of the statesmen host,
Or glance through papers, magazines or watch
The TV, listen to the radio;
Is there the slightest mention of the fact
That rank fanaticism is the main cause
Of this alarming tension, which may end
In a catastrophe for both the sides?

The Russians blame the West for ill designs
And West blames them for malicious aims,
Hundreds of thousand high-rank intellects,
Well paid, well read, discerning and astute,
Highly accomplished in their chosen art,
Conscientious in their duties, born of love
For nation, calm, serene and dignified,
Without suspecting it, pour from their lips,
Dictate to their secretaries or voice
Through media, what are pure, brazen lies,
To justify this or condemn that stand,
Affirm, assert, applaud or else deny,
Denounce, decry in running streams of what

Are only polished forms of pure untruth,
Deceit, prevarication and refuse.

This diabolic ritual of today,
For earthly goods to make a slave of soul,
Most states perform to show the other wrong,
Defeating one another in the attempt
To whitewash their own side and blacken that
Of others, spreading these provocative
And spiteful streams through all the media
To every corner of the weary earth.

The irony is that the masses know
The erstwhile guarded secrets of this trade,
Which every day the media expose,
And people listen to full well-informed
That all what they hear is brainwashing done
By well paid agents of contentious lands.

Sly hints and comments from the listening hosts,
Sometimes abuses, maledictions, too,
Attend these well-prepared relays of news;
A daily pastime of ambitious states,
Regardless of this that the time has passed
To serve this twaddle on the knowing crowds,
Which has the very opposite effect,
Sometimes, of what it is designed to have.
But on the captives of a time-worn rut
The old traditions still maintain their hold,
And need to be discarded, yielding place

To new, solacious methods of exchange
Of greeting 'twixt two nations, if they have
The wish to live in peace and harmony.
The billions spent on this notorious craft
Bring no return, when counted in terms of
Abiding assets—good name, honor, love,
Respect and all of those surpassing gifts,
Which bind two distant nations in the bonds
Of trust and friendship that alone can change
The present tense condition of the world.

There is no gulf between two human hearts
Which cannot be bridged o'er with warming love,
No difference between two human minds
Which wisdom, skill and tact cannot remove,
Or enmity between two nations which
Exceeding love for peace cannot replace
With friendship, if one side is earnest in
The efforts made to end the cleaving feud.
A war becomes inevitable when
There is lack of adjustment on both sides,
Each keen to put the other in the wrong,
Each, like a rough, aggressive to the last,
Each thinking that his honor is at stake
Oblivious to the hazards of the fight.

'Tis not the Russians or Americans,
Most of them, doubtlessly, kind and humane,
Pacific and affectionate at heart
To strangers, hating e'en the name of war

Or, let us say, their vast majority
That is impatient for a bloody fight,
But when excited and brainwashed by
Manipulation of the media,
Or by exaggerating a small mistake,
Their native friendliness is turned to hate.
The task of elders is to heal the young
Of this contagious fever of the mind,
But, far from this, it is they who excite
Their ire to win support for their own plans
By whipping up hysteria in the crowds.

It is the more intelligent human brains
Which, mounting to the top positions in
The many spheres of complex human life,
Made e'en more intricate by science now
By vast additions to few human needs,
Who make use of the high positions gained,
To feed their pride, ambition, greed or hate
In fomenting uprisings which they need
To win objectives, precious in their eyes.
The passive crowds become but handy tools
And, though incited by suggestion, think
That their explosive outburst was their own.
In this now regular exchange of fire,
Between the superpowers, the point is lost:
Why this unholy preparation for
A most annihilative war, what for
This daily barrage of well-dressed tirades

And highly painted falsehoods, coined to wrap
The dirty linen of one round the other;
This growling, barking, snarling every hour;
Which suits a howling, shouting street brawl more
Than a polite exchange of views between
Two foremost nations, e'en though now estranged.

Excuse me for these rather sour remarks,
But if, per chance, you were now in my place,
And saw the sight, which is denied to you,
To what disaster these tirades would lead,
And what unpaintable horror, torment, death
Would come out from these hits on either side,
Leaving a battered, bruised, disabled race
To mourn the wounds and deaths for centuries.

This hideous war is now approaching fast,
Beyond the power of man to avert the blow.
Already the monster hovers o'er the site
Which at the appointed hour the Fire will light.
O, ye encrowned elite of every state,
Tone down your fervor and slow down your pace;
Let not your own descendants take your name
With horror and abhorrence for the pain
And agony that will fall to their lot,
By your impatience, lack of wisdom or
Your want of insight to foresee the end.

For Heaven's sake, retrace your steps before
It is too late, reduce your pressure and

Soften your tone, relax the tense state of
Your mind, slow down the preparations for
A war, abandon fast the nuclear race!

That would make you a greater hero than
If you emerge victorious in the fight,
Which would kill millions and pollute the earth.
Whether you win or lose, the stigma of
The frightful carnage done shall stick to you.
The progeny will argue had you shown
More wisdom, foresight, patience, tact and love
Of nation, you could have avoided war!

O, ye true-hearted folk of every land,
Do not forget the wholesome lessons taught
By history, both present and the past.
No nation on the earth could e'er retain
Her dominant position longer than
A certain period of time after which
It sank down slowly or fell fast to earth,
Depending on how elders steered her craft,
And how far sound in mind the masses were.
You have the example fresh before your eyes
Of Britain, which in only fifty years,
Has lost the greatest empire ever seen,
So vast, on it the sun-god never set.

Remember Hitler, Alexander and
Napoleon, and beware that the same fate
Which overtook them and their countries, too,

Might not befall your nation and yourself,
Exposing you before the progeny,
In all your nakedness as one who cared
More for himself than for the newly born
Whom he exposed, to quench his thirst for power
Or prestige, to such a disgusting life
Of toil, disease and dearth that they detest
His very name for all the torture borne.

Be not a party to an Evil which
Can spell extinguishment of life on earth
And mean insurgence 'gainst the rule of God,
To merit torture with infernal tools.
For Heaven's sake weigh well, before you leap,
The consequences of this mad attempt
To pile up nuclear arms and keep the world
In such a state of stress that they are used.
For nigh two thousand years the words of Christ
And what Buddha enjoined before his time—
Eschewing violence in thought and deed—
Were not accepted by the down-to-earth,
Hard-headed ranks of scholars and the elite—
Machiavelli is a case in point—
As something vital for the life of man,
Something essential for survival and
Ascribed the Sermon to mere fantasy.

But now, unless we act on this advice,
Mankind may come to an ignoble end.
This shows the counsel was perfectly timed,

Through Revelations from the Oversoul,
To warn the race she must prepare herself
For handling Forces, which employed by those
Not skilled in curbing their ambition, greed,
Desire and anger, can destroy the world.
To save the race is to win the applause
Of our descendants for a thousand years;
And he alone shall wear this glorious crown,
Who, by his wisdom, can avert this war.

All those who fight against this awful doom
Have firm religious sanction on their side;
They will be glorified in both the worlds,
This and the next, their conscience clear and bright,
Their triumph: mastery of lower self,
And freeing mankind from the Devil's hold.
Although resourceless, they will be recalled
With honor, love and tears by grateful crowds,
Their names engraved for e'er on loyal hearts
They rescued from the open jaws of death,
By their heroic acts, done at the risk
Of disappointing their pugnacious friends,
Who burn to kindle soon the fires of war.

These words, too, will survive this age for long,
And witness bear to exhortations made
To one and all to eschew the thought of war,
For nuclear engines have now made it what
Our love of life and sanity forbid,
For future wars will not be human wars,

But Devils fighting to ease their itch for
Evil met only in the vilest hell.

This Message shall prove that, with heavenly Grace,
Mortals can win to that clairvoyant state
Where future is revealed to them, at times
Of great emergency, when sudden death
Or grave disaster stares Man in the face.

I know such is the harsh decree of Fate
That these words shall fall on unheeding ears.
The war will soon break out for reasons which
Will be discussed in this inspired discourse.
'Tis not that nature is averse to peace
Or that the heavenly Judge is wrath with man,
For some capricious reason of His own,
Or that there is disorder, lawlessness
And chaos in the Lord's dominion or
That this is but a dead, insentient world,
In which the soul has no existence, or
That earthly life exists by merest chance,
A highly complex product of pure dust.

No, none of these. The true position is
That man has wandered far off from his Path.
Either he should correct his fault himself,
Which is the easiest and the safest way,
Or nature will set him right with her whip
So that he does not miss the Path again!
What else do holy scriptures talk about
When they set hell and damnation for

Departure from the conduct ruled by Faith?
The Drama now unfolding round us is
A vindication of religious Truths.
But since we know not why they were revealed
We fail to see the clearly visible links.

How crafty and corrupt would grow the world,
When e'en religious-minded, simple folk,
The toiling multitudes all o'er the earth,
The young and old, the learned and the raw,
Come to believe they have no soul to own,
There is no God to oversee their deeds,
The world is but a dead, insentient mass
Of energy, some of which by mere chance
Transformed itself into humanity;
And it is widely known that mind is born
Of chemical reaction and that life
In all its forms, reptilian, animal,
Fish, insect, bird and human—children, men
And women who, howe'er intelligent,
Artistic, skillful, charming, good and kind,
Are but organic products, no more than
Random concoctions of a rarer type,
Which vanish into air when bodies die—
A rare effluvium rising from the flesh
To melt away when its reactions cease?

What wide revulsion in thought would occur,
What sorrow and despair would seize the crowds,
What chaos and confusion would prevail

When science finally confirms the view
That there is no hereafter, soul or God,
And human life is but an empty dream:
The fitful light shed by a candle burnt
By nature, with the tender wax of flesh,
To flicker near the end, when worn with age
The weary mind at last, sinks into death,
Extinguished, once for all, to leave behind
The corpse to mingle with the listless earth,
From which it rose to shine but for a while.

A thinking, talking, laughing, grieving flame,
Which, as Man, when alive, had stood erect,
Postured his body, cultivated gait
To look impressive, and adorned his mind
With noble traits, with truth and rectitude,
To accord with his assumed divine descent,
And with the norms of his community.
For he believed in his intrinsic worth
As something pure and lofty, far above
The pools of mud and slush he saw around,
Above well-mixed compounds of pharmacists,
Above decoctions, potions, mixtures, brews,
Above e'en trees and plants, birds, beasts and fish,
Above which all he towered, like a god,
The Monarch of a Kingdom, kept in trim
By Nature with none else to share his crown.

But what will be the state of human hearts,
Of human culture and society,

If for a century this hope is dashed
To ground, and purely godless, soulless crowds
Make merry, eat and drink, in the belief
That they are transient shadows, born of chance,
With no essential binding to keep straight,
And but a narrow span of time to taste
The joys of life and make the fullest use
Of this chance-sent occasion to fulfill
All their desires, ambition, passion, lust;
To love without restraint the prettiest girls,
And win unscrupulously honored heights
To make the prime a hotbed of delight,
With no thought of default or sin or shame.

When moral principles lose all their charm,
For those convinced that life is but a farce,
How can fine scruple grow in bitter minds,
Or tender conscience live in burning hearts?
Who will be keen to honor social norms,
Or higher values, virtue or e'en laws,
Or practise charity, compassion, good,
When human hearts are shorn of love and faith,
And selfish aims and objects reign supreme?
A rising tide of mass corrruption and
Revolt against restraints would overwhelm
The race, and no amount of coercion used
Would help to keep the multitudes in check,
When once the sanctity of human life,
The trust in heaven and faith in God are lost.

A disillusioned and embittered race,
Enfettered by the inexorable laws
Of matter, with no opening for release,
Despite hard efforts, would live on the earth,
With all hope of eternal life destroyed,
All thought of lasting good or values dead,
All faith in soul's divinity belied,
And trust in heavenly justice lost for e'er,
Acutely conscious that what one beholds
As cosmos is a boiling cauldron of
A monstrous force, insensitive to all
That we associate with life and soul,
Entirely dead to love, compassion, truth,
Integrity, uprightness, justice, right,
Sincereness, loyalty or honesty;
The basic principles from which arise
Our jurisprudence, social standards or
The rules and procedures of governments;
The soil on which democracy is grown,
The base on which society is built,
The ground on which our law and order stand,
Which have made mankind what she is today.

What will befall the disenchanted race
If such pernicious doctrines e'er become
The last avowed and proved philosophy
And guide in all the spheres of human life?
What soulless intellects would take the lead,
What heartless leaders would usurp the front,
What godless scholars, teachers, artists, scribes,

Professors, traders or industrialists,
Devoid of conscience, virtue, morals, faith,
Love and compassion would prey on the weak
And helpless, like relentless, hungry sharks,
To push the race back to the savage bourne,
With its inhuman rule of tooth and claw,
Of soulless robots lost to human traits?
Since more than others they will know the truth;
That they are but a momentary flash
Of light to be extinguished for all time,
Like to a candle flame, blown out by wind,
Or the glow of a firefly in the dark,
Which in a moment disappears from sight,
How in the bitterness of shattered dreams
Can they possess the Will or have the Heart
To strive for great ideals of Love and Truth?

JONAH CALLING NINEVAH TO REPENTANCE
Jonah i — iii.

The Book of Jonah begins with the Lord saying, "Arise, go to Ninevah, that great city, and cry against it; for their wickedness is come up before me." The people believe him and repent. A fast is proclaimed. Even the king put on sackcloth and sat in ashes. "And God saw their works, that they turned from their evil way," and Ninevah was spared.

CHAPTER VII

THE WORLD ON THE VERGE OF COLLAPSE

Denial of God, when still the human brain
Is an unfathomed mystery, is like
The claim of one who ne'er has seen a ship,
Narrating loud his voyage round the earth.
The picture of the cosmos in our mind
Is drawn by sensual artists, counting five.
We do not know which is the perfect one
That draws the most correct resemblance of
The basic substance spread out all around,
And which, without their aid, we cannot know,
Nor have the least awareness of, save what
Is brought in by these five door-keepers who
Guard the corporeal prison we live in,
Nor do we know how mind translates their signs,
Made in a language we have never read,
Nor who has coined this language for our use.

Hence what trust can we have in one who claims
Conclusive knowledge of the Universe
But does not know the language in which all
This knowledge is recorded nor the script
In which the language, too, is written down?
Yet boasts that he has made a study of
The whole of literature in that script,
And found no mention of God anywhere?
Or what trust can a child command who thinks
Its home town is the locus of the world,
And that the horizon marks the end of all
The peopled space there is contained in it?
Such are the scholars who pass verdicts on
This vast creation and its primary Cause,
Not knowing that they trespass on a soil
To which they have no title nor least claim!
For matter is but a delusive mist.

Who can say that the Cosmos, save mankind,
Has no superior forms of thinking minds,
With other senses we do not possess,
Which show them quite a different world than that
Our own five sensory organs show to us?
How do we know the mirror of our mind
Does not distort the image we perceive
And, all our life, we live as captives in
Our body, guarded by five sentinels,
Which ne'er allow our mind to by-pass them
To see the outer world as it exists?

The first birth-pangs of communism began

When science was much younger than it is
Today, and savants thought the world was made
Of solid particles of matter. But
This theory, now an old, exploded myth,
Has lost its former place among the wise.
The volume of our knowledge has since grown
By leaps and bounds, to such dimensions that,
Compared to it, the stockpile at that time
Was but a spur compared to a mountain now.

Some myths have been exposed, some new ones framed:
The sky, the ocean, water, air and earth,
Seen through the eyes of scientists, are now
So full of wonders and fresh riddles that
The scholars of that era, one might say,
Lived in old-fashioned huts and drove in carts,
In contrast to the mansions and the cars
Of our day; but were so conceited that
They thought they had attained the highest rung
Of knowledge to which intellect can climb;
A common failing of the human mind,
More so among the learned who, shut up
Inside the prison of their time, believe
The last word on their subject has been said—
The same old fallacy, the mother of
Inflexible dogma, heaven's recurring curse
On vanity and pride of knowledge which
Obstructs the otherwise smooth path of wit,
And which is as tenacious now as it
Was at the time when Marx announced his creed.

Denial of God by man, as old as hills,
Is but the product of conceited minds
That lack subtility and thought profound
To plumb the awesome ocean of this theme.
The views expressed by Marx about the then
Prevailing concepts of theistic faiths,
Were borrowed from some scholars of the time,
Including Darwin, Huxley and the rest,
Who ne'er knew where their rash attempt would lead
Once borrowed they became the pillar of
His ideology, upheld today
By nearly half the dwellers on the earth,
Most of whom, ne'er sufficiently informed
About the later vast additions to
Our knowledge, still hold rigidly to what
Is but a notion, not a proven fact,
Which further data is dislodging now.
But for the communist, this creed is still
As sacred as it was when first proclaimed.

A striking parallel between the faiths
Of old and Soviets' blank denial of God
Is that the methods used are nigh the same—
The patronage of state, espionage,
Brainwashing, propaganda, dogma and
Repression, e'en the rod at times of need.

So there can be no doubt about the fact
That, notwithstanding their dismissal of
Religion as a hurdle in the way

Of progress, Soviets, too, profess a creed,
As firmly and dogmatically as do
Fanatical adherents of a faith.
What clearly marks their rupture with the West
Is their unalterable denial of God,
In whom the West believes, though there, too, now
Among the learned skepticism prevails,
And dogma, which inflexibly adheres
To what is still unproven and in doubt.

This feud would soon end in a tragedy
That would drain off the venom from both sides,
Remove the clouds of dogma and conceit
Which, sometimes, need misfortune to dispel.
Too oft dogmatic scholars scatter views,
Which, though mistaken, when exploited by
The clever, for their ends, become the cause
Of serious ills for the believing crowds.

A common ruse of politicians is
They often make use of a popular tide
To ride on opponents, to win a name,
And find a safe niche in the peoples' hearts.
Manipulation of this handy tool
Is a must in the art of statesmanship.
The common people often dearly pay
For cherished views, beliefs and sentiments,
Which oft provide the peg on which to hang
Their talk for more astute and clever brains
That prey on the sincerity of crowds.

The madness fostering this crisis is
On both the sides, one shut from Faith and God,
For which there is no soul or hereafter,
No Judgment for its actions here or there;
The type of talent now more common in
The world, both in the rich and poorer lands,
For which no man-made law can ever act
As a deterrent to make it refrain
From plans and aims, which always center round
Its own objectives, out of which arise
The actions done to make its dreams come true.

It is this class of men and women who,
When at the top of a profession, trade
Or government, by their dogmatic views
And stubborn will, invite disaster for
Themselves and those whom they profess to serve.

The world is on the verge of a collapse,
Because there is no agreement between
The scholars and the statesmen of the earth,
No point on which the major part agrees;
No target which most of them would work for,
No summit to which most would like to rise,
No faith to which the skeptics could subscribe,
And no ideals all would like to share
To mold their life and conduct in that form.
But, on the contrary, most have their pets
Among the actors, boxers, athletes,
Or statesmen, scholars, stuntmen, scientists,

Reformers, saints, professors, artists, priests,
Magicians, witches, drug addicts or crooks,
Whom they their models make to imitate.

The riddle is how educated minds,
Which know well that the existence of a God
Has not been proved, till now, nor e'en disproved,
That same is the case with the Human Soul,
The same with After-life, the same with Faith,
And many other problems, still unsolved.
The same, too, with the goal of human life,
Can be so obstinate on either side,
So much fanatical in their beliefs,
And so dogmatic in their passing views
That split up into two disputing camps,
For what precisely, it is hard to say,
The two are girding up fast their loins for
A fight to total death on either side;
A fight so dreadful that a hundred years
Would not suffice to abate its stabbing pain.

For our debate, let us suppose, a while,
This suicidal split in all the race
Is based on issues which are still unsolved;
For instance, issue of the human soul,
Or of the after-world, or God and Faith,
Or of the real goal of human life,
Or similar issues all unsettled yet,
Or communism and private enterprise,
Which all can be bilaterally discussed

And settled by the leaders of the two.
Where then exists the need to fight a war?
Would it be sane to make these issues such
Important points of honor, that call for
The sacrifice of country, home and life,
Or for a war hysteria to defend
One's ideology e'en at the cost
Of all the nation and all life on earth?
Who would recommend such a crazy course?

But these are not the only problems left
To be decided. There are others, too.
For instance, what is the most healthy mode
Of life which mankind must adopt to gain
The greatest satisfaction from her stay
On earth, the greatest peace and happiness?
And what the most becoming social order,
To keep the human mass in lasting bonds
Of love, peace, liberty and brotherhood,
So that each member of the race may feel
Contented with his portion and derive
The greatest joy and profit from his life?

There is no doubt that scholars, on both sides,
Are doing all they can to answer these
Unanswered riddles, but that may take time.
But in the meanwhile we must all behave
With patience and forbearance to avoid
Collisions over trifles that make us

Like children fighting in the classroom, when
The teacher is not there to keep them calm.
Knowing that every system now in use,
And every life-style, whether of the East
Or West, and e'en the belief in God or Soul,
Are tentative, considered in the light
Of our prevailing knowledge of the world,
No scholar, statesman, scientist or priest
Can say with confidence that he has found
The answer to these riddles that can stand
The acid test of time or which can win
Acceptance from the learned of all grades.

So we are left with this conclusion that
There are still bristling problems which demand
Solution to allow mankind to know
How she should live, how organise herself
Into societies or single states,
And what she should believe about herself,
Her destination, how to achieve it and
The nature of her Soul and what is God.

In both the rival powers, which stand arrayed
For war, a bulky part of each which runs
Into tens of millions, may be, e'en a third
Of total populations, does not see
Eye to eye with the o'er-all policy
Of their own nations, but submit, perforce,
To what the large majority decides.
Nor all the people of these countries feel

That they receive in full what they deserve
Or are as fairly treated as the rest;
Nor e'en the leaders of these states agree
Among themselves or hold the same ideals,
Or are unanimous in thought and deed.
The only reason why they all unite,
At times of crises, is because the men
In power decide to take that step and pull
The strings to make the nation one with them.

So it is not political ideals
Nor life-styles, nor religion, nor belief,
Nor e'en the thought that nation is in risk,
That drives a country to a disastrous war,
But oft the machination of a few
Who use these shibboleths to arouse the mass.
No nation can convince most of the world
That her own ideology, beliefs,
The way of life or social structure is
The best on earth, proved by the test of time,
Or by experiment: So why this stress
On their ideals by the opposing camps,
Like vendors loudly selling fancy goods?

Then why this rivalry, dissension, war,
This vast expenditure on armaments,
This preparation for a ghastly fight,
Which may turn these lands into sepulchres;
This swollen flood of propaganda lies,
These demonstrations, protest meetings, fights

By people who oppose the policy?
Why should this happen, when the men at top,
If they choose, can put out the smoking fire,
Before the flames unite to cause a blaze
That cannot be extinguished any more?

It does not stand to reason, they cannot
Because the last decision rests with them,
And 'tis they who interpret all the moves,
Survey the data, read the documents,
And analyse the whole position ere
Taking decisions on behalf of all
The nation to plunge it into war or,
Avoiding that, let it abide in peace.
The reason for resorting to a war
Does not rest on the rivals' creed, belief,
Their ideology or way of life,
But on self-interest, obsession 'gainst
The rival, prejudice, fear of attack
Or loss of prestige, trade, resources, wealth,
Or a predominant position in
The world, or but a crazy frame of mind,
Which thirsts for war or hates someone to death.

There are some other reasons, too, besides
The ones detailed, that caused wars in the past.
For instance, thirst for more dominion or
Possession, plunder, treasure, women, slaves,
Sometimes religion and fanaticism.
This makes it clear that now, as in the past,

A war erupts, not for the reasons that
Are oft assigned for it, but always, with
Some rare exceptions, just because the likes,
Dislikes, desires and passion, hopes and fears
Ambitions, aspirations, greed and lust
Come into play, as they did in the past,
As they do in most way-side quarrels and
In every form of conflict anywhere.

Divested of their horror, modern wars
Are no more than rehearsals of the past,
With this distinction that instead of one—
A king or chief—may be a hundred take
The last steps in deciding they would fight.
But in this hundred, too, the voice of but
A few prevails in winning o'er the rest.
A nation of a hundred million is
Thus drawn into a vortex by the will
Of but a handful, who pretend that what
They did had the support of everyone,
To flatter people they, too, had a hand
In what was settled by the topmost few.

Since this is how democracy controls
The state, the handful on the top do not
Have any other option to unite
The nation, both in war and peace, except
With well-tried tools and methods now in use.
Whether unfair or fair, untrue or true,
Unchaste or pure, they are to be employed,

As safety of the state is paramount.
This is a logic no one can dispute,
And it went very well throughout the past.
The top men, certainly, have no course left,
When dealing with the public, which includes
The evil-minded and the sadist lot,
The whole fraternity of criminals,
The circles of self-seekers, egotists,
Abnormals, cracks, insurgents and the rest.
How else can they control this motley crowd?

But ruling o'er a country and the art
Of statesmanship to win potential foes,
Or of commanding the trust of the world,
Or acting as a leading power on earth,
Or as a dominant one for the good
Of all, are not identical and need
Divergent methods to achieve the end.

A new-born factor has now come into play
And made the task much harder than before;
For statesmen and the ruling hierarchies,
Who wish to steer their countries safely through
The cataracts and rapids in the way,
In dealing with all nations of the earth.
And this new factor is the nuclear arm,
With which no one had to contend before,
Which has now changed the whole image of war
To pose the greatest problem for the wit
Of man to solve with safety by her skill.

Under the pretext of their passion for
Promoting friendship, love and peace among
The nations, why is there this sinister game,
On both the sides, of winning o'er this state
Or that one, played with pawns, picked out with care
And paid exorbitantly for their part—
The most nefarious and depraved on earth—
With full permission of the leading ranks,
That ne'er confess to what is honest Truth?
They are the inciters and abettors of
The blackest felonies e'er done by man,
While all the time professing to uphold
Love, kindness, fair play, truth and probity—
A state of mass confusion which condones
These crimes as serving nations' interests:
A most pernicious doctrine aimed to keep,
Subject to human choice, the Moral Laws.

What good can come out of this guilty sport,
In which the superpowers are busy in
A kind of competition aimed to woo
The sister nations to take up their cause:
A bloody race, when judged from its results,
In which the two fanatically uphold
Their ideologies and systems for
All countries of the earth to copy from,
To join this or that block to have the pride
Of place among the communists or with
Their rivals, capitalists, as they choose?
We know too well the folk on either side

Are not convinced that their ideals are
The choicest, viable for all time to come.
But still the elite on both sides try so hard
To foist their system on the other states—
Many of them unwilling to oblige—
With filthy methods which too oft result
In riots, bloodshed and destruction in
The countries not disposed to adopt their ways.

A most abhorrent, subtle game of chess
Is played on every square of the chessboard
Of earth, with moves and countermoves, before
The watchful eyes of shrewd spectators who
At once detect the hidden hand behind
A move and often curse the players who,
To serve their country, try to ruin theirs—
A filthy chapter in the annals of
Our time to which our children shall ascribe
Some of the horror we invite for them.

What else can come out of the dramas staged
In many luckless, poorer lands in which
Uprisings, riots, and rebellions,
Disputes and conflicts are manoeuvered fast
With bribes, incentives, lavish use of funds,
Corruption, blackmail, girls, allurements, drugs
And every foul device, betrayal, fraud,
Deceit, abduction, murder, massacre,
And every vice and crime condemned by Faith,
Abhorred by man, forbidden by the laws,

Both man-made and Divine which, in their zeal
To beat the other side, the mightiest states
On earth are using secretly to foul
The name of kindness, love, humanity,
And to misuse the terms ideology,
Freedom, equality and human rights,
Or brotherhood and proletariat,
For what are, when unmasked, ignoble aims.

So how can we explain this paradox:
The true foundation of all systems of
Government, and their ideologies,
Or what they hold essential for the good,
The peace and joy of their compatriots,
Are truth, uprightness, honesty and all
The virtues stressed by Faith and all the wise
Who e'er arose in Russia or the West?
How then in almost all ascendant states
There is a full reversal of this rule
To gain inglorious ends and selfish aims,
Dominion, precedence, resources, wealth?

How can the world abide in lasting peace
When we employ, to hit a rival hard,
Nefarious methods and infamous means,
While harping on our virtues all the time?
If not this moment then some other day
A war must needs erupt to end this sham.

One great misfortune is our serious lack
Of fuller knowledge of organic life

And mind, as they are both beyond the probe
Of all our senses, e'en the intellect.
We cannot see the Source from which they spring:
The boundless ocean of terrestrial mind,
Which both surrounds and penetrates the globe,
A Sea of energy that has no shore,
Nor shape nor form, resembling our own minds,
Which we can neither touch nor hear nor see,
But not embodied nor conditioned by
The senses, but pure mind existing far
And wide, so concentrated, so profound
And so intelligent that language fails.
From this reservoir of terrestrial mind
Come all our thoughts, ideas, notions or
Discoveries and inventions, skills and arts,
Also the weird phenomena produced
Through mediums and psychics by a force
We know nothing about, whose frolic is
What we see spellbound in a seance room,
Unconscious all the while that our own dreams
And fancies are made of that very stuff.

It is this Ocean of Intelligence
Which, acting through the leading brains involved,
Controls the mental climate of the earth.
Thus, when the Eternal Laws which rule the Fate
Of mankind are defied, conducing to
Distortion in the thinking and the acts
Of nations or their institutions or
Their leaders, statesmen, writers, teachers, priests,

To heal the chronic ailment, there arrives
Calamity, which with a bitter dose
Of pain and suffering cures the sickly mind.

Existence of the nuclear engines is
A challenge to the Powers-that-be of earth,
An insult to the very name of Right
And buffet in the face of every Faith.
What can involve extinction of the race,
Like nuclear stockpiles, ready now for use,
Implies a plan so heinous and profane,
E'en if there is no thought to push it through,
A notion so inhuman and unclean
There is no word for it in any tongue,
A thinking so insane that e'en among
The maddest there can be no one so mad.

Where is the sanction from religion or
The Lord or man-made laws or conscience
Or international justice or e'en from
The constitutions of the nuclear states
For an infernal engine of this kind?
Where is provision in the rules observed
In warfare from beginning to the day,
When this, till then unheard of, foul device
Was first employed to kill civilians,
Unweaponed, unprepared and innocent?

How did the practice of mass murder start,
And killing of civilians become

A now accepted feature of warfare?
Where is the inter-state decision or
An agreement adopted by the world
To use this deadly blight in future wars?
'Tis all an unbecoming, shifty game
Of superpowers, unmindful of the end,
To thrust a cursed contrivance on the world;
And keep themselves and all the race in fear
Of death, destruction, lethal injuries
Or cureless ailments for all time to come.

For Heaven's sake, O, ye much-honored chiefs,
Ye brilliant penmen and ye great elite
Of every clime and country on the earth,
Forbear, and let not your ambitious plans
For more dominion, prestige, markets, wealth,
Resources, domination or revenge,
Pervert your thinking and subvert your will,
And losing sight of what a war would cost,
When fought with nuclear engines, pray restrain
Your ardor and in calmer moments ask
Yourself: How can you gain your cherished ends
If, only after a few hours of fight
With missiles, earth would be a wilderness,
And all that on which you now build your plans
Dissolve into air, like a vanished dream,
And you will find yourself, if still alive,
The monarch of the waste surrounding you!

ELIJAH'S ASCENT IN A CHARIOT OF FIRE
II Kings ii.

The closing scene in the life of the great prophet, so wrapped up in startling and extraordinary events, was more marvellous and impressive than any other presented: "And it came to pass when the Lord would take up Elijah into heaven by a whirlwind."

CHAPTER VIII

THE SUPREME OBJECTIVE
TO BE WON

Let us begin now with a fleeting look
At those commercial markets of our day
Where honor, truth and honesty are sold
At prices suited to the pockets of
The buyers and the needs of vendors both;
The market which was founded when mankind
Achieved such heights in knowledge, art and science,
As none had e'er dreamt of in all the past.
None had conceived that such heights could exist,
That man can be the prince he is today,
The humblest, too, commanding such delights,
Which monarchs in the past could never taste
Nor e'en imagine in their royal dreams.

The movies, TV's, phones and radios,
Computers, automobiles, aeroplanes,
Electric light, pipe-water, transport and
The other luxuries, available now

To both the rich and poor, in olden times
Were all beyond the dreams of mighty kings.
In e'en the premier empires of the past,
In Eygpt, India, China, Greece and Rome,
The richest ne'er had what the poor have now,
Or what they can command, whene'er they like,
They ne'er had such cures for the ills of flesh,
Nor such sedatives to relieve their pain
Nor e'en such chances to prolong their life
Or keep themselves immune from pestilence.
Man ne'er had e'en a tithe of all the ware
Which science has now pressed into his hands!

Amid this rank profusion of all that
Is needed for a long and healthy life
Of peace and happiness, amusement, sport,
Abundance, luxury, fun, frolic, thrill,
There should not have been e'en the slightest sign
Of war or violence, of vice or crime,
Revolt, aggression, plunder or deceit.
But from what is transpiring, o'er the earth,
It seems that Wrong is triumphing o'er Right,
That Evil is victorious over Good,
And Vice is trampling Virtue, for today
The good, the simple and the honest souls
Are treated as surviving fossils of
A prediluvian species which believed
In Godhead only to deceive itself,
And drug the intellect with opium,
So that it failed to see the cruel side

Of life, the crushing blows of Nature in
Upheavals, earthquakes, famines, floods and droughts,
Extremes of weather, blizzards and typhoons,
Disease, disasters, ills and plagues galore,
All born of love and mercy of the Lord,
From His Compassion and Benevolence—
The picture drawn of Him by theist faiths.

Equipped with these convincing arguments,
Drest in the richest language of the day,
The great exponents of atheistic creeds,
Unmindful of the havoc they would cause,
With all the implements and tools in hand,
Provided nimbly by advancing science,
Soon razed to earth the edifice of faith
And excommunicated God Himself
From the society of scholars, their
Academies and universities,
Also from the select community
Of high-grade talent and bright intellect,
In diverse busy spheres of human life,
Who e'en if loyal soon became averse
To owning it for fear of ridicule
From their confreres who outnumber them.
And so kept mum about their true beliefs.

Assent to this expulsion also came
From administrations and good governments,
From commerce, industry, art, business, trade
And, lastly, e'en from countless homes and hearths,

Leaving the folk to do whate'er they like,
A happy riddance, for He poked His nose
Into the private lives of honest folk
By His demanding worship of Himself—
A host of ceremonies and rituals with
Confessions and repentance all designed
To keep the faithful firmly in His grip,
Curtailing freedom of the fold in thought
And deed, against the norms of liberty.

The stalwarts of the Church, like Wilberforce,
The Brahmins, Mullahs, Lamas and the Priests,
Were silenced easily, when threatened with
The weapons forged by the elite of science,
Like Darwin and the rest, disproving that
The Lord of Heaven could ever have a hand
In man's appearance on this planet or
In his unmatched ascent to intellect,
A most incredible feat performed by earth,
With sunlight, air and water, all combined,
Without direction from a Sapient Head,
Producing what they proudly call themselves,
The One Organic Wonder which e'er graced
The world—this self-conceited, erring man,
Who now with his hand on the trigger waits
The signal, like a fool, to shoot himself,
On issues so inane that, calmly weighed,
They would make him the laughing stock of all
The man-like species in the Universe.

The ouster of religion and denial
Of God set up a void they had to fill,
To find a substitute to place before
The crowds to worship and adore, with heart
And soul, to press hard to their bosoms and
Make it the main incentive and chief cause
For every effort done and task performed,
For every single articulated word,
And every thought embodied in a book,
For every mock expression on the face,
And every sign or gesture with the hands,
Or eyes or eyebrows, mouth, lips, nose or tongue,
Or postures of the body on a stage;
In short, which could enthuse, inspire or spur
The people to apply themselves with all
The power of their endurance, wit and skill
To do their daily chores or special tasks.

The learned and the raw, on searching round
To find a surrogate to act for God,
And all what e'er religion had upheld
As the supreme objective to be won,
After a long chase, hit upon, at last,
A lustrous metal of a yellow hue,
Shining, when burnished, and immune from rust,
Used for adornment, idols, ornaments,
Imperial crowns and coins throughout the past—
A worthy symbol of great purity,
Divine grace, affluence and royalty,
They placed it on the high pedestal which,

Reserved by Faith for God, was vacant now,
Since waiting to receive an occupant
To hold before the eyes of eager crowds
As their new sovereign to whom they must bow,
Hold dearer e'en than life, more precious than
Character, principles, religion, truth.

With great rejoicing, fanfare and eclat,
The cherished Idol was installed in place;
And with the beat of drums adherents told
To adore and worship it, without a stop,
Carry its likeness in their pockets, so
That they do not forget to pray to it,
Whene'er they meet misfortune on the way,
Or there arises inescapable need,
When, like a talisman, it comes to life
To overcome the one and meet the other.
A humanistic God who all at once
Responds to prayer and bestows the boon
Sought for, in this respect excelling far
The living God, who never cares to move
His little finger to save devotees
From grave afflictions, e'en when daily prayed
For years, vouchsafing not the least response.

It is a symptom of inertia
Or mental lethargy if one declines
To make a thorough search with all his skill
Into the causes keeping all the world
In such a state of fix, uncertain how
The tussle 'twixt the superpowers would end.

Trust not the fellow who pleads lack of time
To give due thought to such a vital task,
Nor him who, bustling with too high a sense
Of his importance, deigns no answer, for
'Tis certain that the two are busy in
Unceasing worship of the Mammon God,
Who, vested with unbound, despotic power
By man's cupidity, has now become
A cruel tyrant, so inhuman that
He does not care a fig if millions die
For want of food and millions fall a prey
To mortal ails for lack of medicines,
But rumbles, like a monster, on his way,
Crushing uncounted millions with his weight.

Through all the hoary past, this smiling god
Of fortune-hunters everywhere has been
The one-without-a-second author of
The greatest tragedies which struck mankind,
And mowed down multitudes, like sheaves of corn,
Left millions mutilated in pools of blood,
And millions ravaged, homeless, plundered of
Whate'er they had—possession, honor, wealth—
To live the life of paupers to the end,
Or beg or sell their virtue for a meal.
It is again this god who patronized
The cruelest massacres and butcheries,
Which turned gay cities into cemeteries,
Or peopled regions into wilderness,
With only vermin and some reptiles left.

The worst rebellions, mutinies, revolts
That shook a blooming country to its roots,
Butchered the high and mighty of the land—
To leave a gruesome story of the events
For the posterity to ponder on
The drama and the actors, who performed
The horrid parts to soak the land in blood
Of both the guilty and the innocent—
Have all originated from the same
Enchanter who, by prompting the "have-nots,"
Made them rise in revolt against the "haves,"
To vent their fury and appease their hate,
For nature has decreed that man shall not
Live in peace till there is a gulf of hate
Between one and the other. For the race,
On her way to a glorious Kingdom, must
Unite in love to make the hard ascent.

Whene'er a grave disaster hit the race
In one part of the planet or the other,
Caused by the slaughter and the ravage done
By sadist kings, ambitious generals or
Adventurous nations with imperial aims,
The motive was the same, at least, among
The rank and file of the marauding hordes:
Despoilment, pillage, loot to grab whate'er
They could catch hold of during the affray,
To make it theirs and, when back in their homes,
To gloat o'er all the plundered treasure and
The goods they were now rich enough to buy.

The scourge of buccaneering, piracy,
Of highway robbery and banditry,
Of thuggee and dacoity that has been
The heinous cause of butcheries untold,
Of suffering, torture, destitution, want,
Captivity and grinding slavery,
Which 'tis beyond the power of pen to paint.
It is a narrative of human brutes,
Who run their spears through babies, torture kids,
Rape murdered women, wear skullgarlands round
Their necks, and lack nigh every human trait,
Save that the incentive for the atrocious crimes,
In them, too, is the same—the lust for gold!

Seldom does history in clear-cut terms
Depict the main cause of man's greatest woes:
The source of deadly pests which claim the lives
Of millions in all parts of earth each year;
The master crook behind those guilty of
The murders, horrors and the havoc caused
By gangsters, robbers, bandits, thieves and cheats,
By secret agents, spies, guerillas, roughs,
Hijackers, terrorists and all the vile,
Detestable tribes whose livelihood depends
On murder, slaughter, robbery and theft,
Or some daredevil gamble which involves
Harassment, suffering deaths and loss untold
To millions of bereaved and ravaged folk;
Who ne'er know that the real cause behind
Their ordeals is what they, too, adore—
The god of fortune and abundance—gold.

The very revolution 'gainst the rule
Of capitalism which, for many years,
Took such a heavy toll of victims and
Led to such horrors and atrocities
That one's bone marrow is chilled at the thought,
Was no less the work of the yellow god,
For their contention was: Divide the wealth,
Which but few own, among the multitudes,
So that the need of everyone is met;
A specious plea, as need can be restrained
To what is meet and healthy for the race,
Without exciting hate or envy in
The part to which due portion is denied;
Without despoiling earth of metal ores
Or other wealth required for future use,
Or swelling basic needs to such degree
That their procurement all one's time consumes,
And makes of man a slave to flesh alone,
A well-fed beast of burden on its rounds.

And what about the legions richly paid
To spy on citizens and daily hunt
For victims, but to swell the labor camps
And prisons, far away in icy belts,
Where myriads live in torment all their life,
To keep the people firmly in the grip,
So that subdued by terror they do not
Uprise against the communist regime?
Again the bounteous god of wealth at work
To keep the strong in power and weak suppressed;

A state so far off from equality
As the north pole is distant from the south.
Though most of them may have the same to eat,
But what about the mental torture borne?
Which is more harmful for health of the two,
A half-filled belly or a fettered mind?
Whate'er the motive—want, love of a cause,
Struggle for freedom, patriotism or
Adventure, itch for vice, daredevilry
Or pure revenge—not a step can be made,
Not a thing done without the active help
Of this one patron saint of all those who
Take to the path of evil with some aim.

It is this ceaseless itch for heaps of gold
Which brought the British first to India
For trade and, later on, with strategy
And lavish use of the same magic stuff,
To buy support, mercenaries and arms,
Made the subcontinent their empire for
A hundred years, enriching their own land
With what they could extract demurely with
Ingenious methods, easy to apply
To subject lands suppressed and firmly ruled.

It is the gold disbursed and thirst for wealth
That drove mercenaries to risk their lives
And man the ships of brave Columbus, who
First sailed from Europe to America.

Alluring stories of the fabulous wealth
Existing in the new-found continent,
Waiting for anyone to make his own,
Excited the imagination of
The needy and the brave with golden dreams
Of a rich Eldorado they must share.
And so some drawn by need, some lured by love
Of bold adventure and some forced to leave
Their countries, swelled into a flooded stream
Of immigrants who turned the virgin soil
Into a heaven and founded what is now
The most advanced and powerful realm on earth;
A dreamland well provided by nature with
A rich abundance of resources that
Can keep the state in plenty, joy and peace;
And make of it the leading power on earth,
Not by aggression nor by show of wealth,
But by the chaste desire to help the rest
In meeting frugal needs, and learning how
To live in comfort, peace and happiness.

Unbounded wealth or what it can achieve
Acts like a poison on the human brain.
It blunts the sense of one's dependance on
His effort and hard work to meet his needs,
And grants unbridled freedom to the mind
To do or think of only what it likes,
Defeating Nature's plan that everyone
Must earn his bread with the sweat of his brow;
The sweat of honest planning, honest toil

And honest listening to the word of God,
To strive, to grow, to prosper and to rise,
But not to slave oneself to death to hoard.
The chaste ideals, stressed by every faith,
Of human life refer to goodness, love,
Compassion, kindness and nobility,
Uprightness, justice, loyalty and truth.
In this select array uplifting man
From animals, who has inducted this
Abject surrender to the god of wealth?

How do the champions of every faith,
Who thunder in the temple, church or mosque,
Expounding loud the doctrines of their creed,
Explain this wild departure from the Path
Prescribed by all great founders of true faiths,
By Buddha, Krishna, Christ, Mohammad and
The other prophets and enlightened seers?
Who has endorsed this triple gate to hell,
To graft, corruption, competition, strife,
Contention, rivalry, deception, fraud,
Extortion, blackmail, robbery and theft,
Dispute, disharmony, disruption, feud,
Conceit, inflation, self-aggrandizement,
Indulgence, luxury, licentiousness,
Distaste for honest work, sloth, indolence,
Insane thirst for possession, morbid greed
And every sin and wrong under the sun,
The cause behind most crimes committed and
Every temptation to which flesh is prone?

Where is e'en one illustrious name among
The most exalted humans ever born,
Acknowledged by the world as masters in
Some art or science or philosophy,
Whose counsels have been heard with reverence,
Who has recommended the pursuit of wealth,
Excessive holdings, ease or pleasure as
The end-all and be-all of human life?
Is this the goal prescribed for the devout
By Faith, the purpose for which man exists,
That after his aeonian climb, he should
Now scatter all the wisdom he has learnt
In this colossal span of time to winds,
And slither back to what he was before;
A beast, devoting all his time and sense
To eat his belly full, to mate and sleep,
Without a moment's pause to turn his mind
And dwell a little on the problem of
His life, for which the brute has not the wit;
But man, who has, when he shirks from the task,
Displays the lack of that essential trait,
One only, which lifts him up from the beast.

In this inventive age of daily floods
Of new devices, gadgets, novelties,
No one knows how this crazy notion took
Root in the minds of both the learned and
The masses, that technology provides
The answer to all problems of mankind,
Can make a paradise of earth and keep

The race in plenty, joy and harmony.
Do we not see the verdant spring of this
Unsafe direction of the human wit
In all the crises which face us today:
Contest between the nations to control
The vanishing resources of the earth—
The fuels, metals, minerals and ores
To feed the huge industrial monsters which
Now gird mankind with hills and dales of steel,
In place of nature's charming vistas, and
Pollute the earth, the air and water so
That man is daily poisoned in his home.

Reflect well on the justice of the Lord,
O friend, and mark how it surpasses all
We can conceive of, or how it transcends
Our intellect to grasp the working of
Inscrutable Laws Divine, how it excels
All systems of our law and justice or
How our digressions from the Path ordained
Are tried impartially by our own Self;
How we accuse, arraign and judge ourselves,
And, at the end, inviolate verdicts pass.
These, too, are executed with no loss
Of time, by us, unconscious all the while
That we are made the instruments to enforce
The judgement passed—to reap the profit or
To pay the penalty for actions done
By us, with purpose, whether right or wrong.
A self-correcting system, like our flesh,

Our mind and intellect, too, heal themselves,
When gripped by false, delusive phantoms of
Imperious power, prestigious wealth or lust
Beyond the limits set by heavenly Laws:
All foul distempers of the mind which stand
As hurdles in the upward climb of Soul.

We have diverted all our love to gold,
Made it the summum bonum of our life,
The pole-star of our effort and our thought,
The God whom we all heart and soul adore,
The Idol we keep in the safest shrine,
The apple of our eye, the dearest pet
That has seduced us from the duty owed
To God, humanity and our own soul,
From chaste ideals and great principles,
From almost every precept of our Faith;
For it commands our time, attention, care,
More than good character and morals both:
The pride and glory of ascendant states
That hold their stately head high in the world,
Conscious of their position as the most
Advanced and wealthy nations on the earth,
Assured that these criteria would be used
Fore'er to assess the greatness of a land;
Assured of their secure position, too,
As the most powerful nations of our day.
In short, by counting on this slippery god,
They ride full tilt against the prayers made
By their religion that 'tis not the way

For mortals to achieve success in life,
If they take Revelation as their guide.

But lo, the same enchanting god of wealth,
Abundance, pleasure, luxury and love,
Our pride and glory, high estate and might;
The hero of all we have e'er achieved,
For whose sake we renounce our hope of heaven,
Of our redemption and our after-life,
Forgetful of our worship, is now deep
In preparations for the approaching war,
Expending lavishly to heap and heap
The most expensive faggots on the pyre,
Now set to roast mankind with all her breed.

The more we have the greater is the chance
To buy the most expensive goods of war—
The most destructive missiles, cannon, tanks,
And all the mammoth host of modern arms,
Which can destroy a country in an hour,
If an intense surprise attack is made.
The more our assets, the more we can spend
To employ the largest army personnel,
To have more bases, ports and launching sites,
To own more ships, submarines and jet planes,
Or largest-e'er industrial complex, with
Delivery systems built to keep full pace
With the demands from numerous battlefronts;
To finance secret operations aimed
To cause disruption in a hostile land.

With this we throw a challenge to the foe
To act as fast and spend as lavishly
To encircle and confront us with the same
Combating might, with armies, missiles, guns
And spies, sufficient now to swallow both.

Remember every empire in the past
Was wrecked by its own o'er-abundance and
By its own wealth, employed by the elite
In mad pursuits of flesh and vain attempts
To win more territory, to gain more wealth,
Until they toppled down amid the cries
Of shame, derision and scorn from the world—
An old phenomenon which might be soon
Repeated, if not guarded against in time—
A wholesome lesson, which so often taught
By nature in the dim past, has not proved
Effective yet in holding greedy man
Back from this most pernicious hunt for gold.
The pet we fondle still against the Law,
Dictates of Faith and lessons of the past,
Now turned into a Demon, threatens us
With death, but still we fail to mend our fault.

'Tis hard to accept that Cosmic Laws of Life
Are so unfathomable and so profound,
So operative through aeonian spans
Of time that intellect reels with the weight
Of problems and their answers, showing how
We, singly or collectively, reward

Ourselves or punish, as decreed by Law.
Think on how this Golconda has been won
And you will see the answer written large
On our now morbid thirst for total wars
To be disabled, killed or burnt alive,
As they do to the denizens of hell
Or those convicted of most heinous crimes
On earth, in either case to uphold the Laws,
Both human and divine, to keep the Soul
On its ascending Path from which it falls,
At times, enticed by cravings of the flesh.

THE DELUGE

Genesis vii.

Because of the wickedness of the people, the rising water of the Flood
overwhelmed the world, engulfing and destroying all living, all breathing
things. The remorseless powers of nature churned unrestrained.

CHAPTER IX

THE FATAL VENOM
SPREADING UNRESTRAINED

Compared to what our nuclear arsenals
Forbode for man, his progeny and world,
All he has done, achieved and stored, so far,
Is negligible before the awesome power,
Which can wipe off mankind, and all she has
Amassed, with but a fraction of the stock
In hand, in but a day, demanding of
The dazed and stunned survivors to make good
With hard and sweating labor, once again,
The loss of ages of unceasing toil.
Remember that this means these weapons have
The power of life and death for all the race—
For her discoveries, culture, arts and crafts,
Possessions, cities, towns, her homes and hearths—
Can lift her to imperial heights of power,
Or dash down to the depths of slavery,
Which might fall to the lot of weaker lands,
If stronger are allowed to act unchecked
In piling up the stuff, as they do now.

It is amazing how, with all this threat
Of catastrophic nuclear battles in
The days to come, with instant total death
Of all of us, the media, as if
Bewitched, refuse to move out of the rut,
And play the monster down to suit their choice,
Their policy, the time available and
The leisure of their editors and chiefs;
So that it nowise interferes in what
They wish to do at their own will and choice.

One hardly can say how they would react
To a certain situation that may rise;
For many considerations come between
What can be done and what they choose to do:
A sly autonomous body which, too prone
To criticise the world, resents the least
Aspersion on its own integrity;
And has become too autocratic now
To be a safe companion for mankind.
But readers slave to habit have no choice,
Except to skip through, with their morning tea,
The daily papers all fresh with the news;
A remnant of the post-Victorian days,
Which, though the world has changed a lot since then
By counting on a habit, does not change.
And may continue acting the same way
Until exploding missiles end its role
To draw the crowds out of a habit, which
Continued endlessly becomes disease.

'Tis for this reason, too, that nature acts,
At times, to cause disruption in our life,
When we contrive our own imprisonment,
Like fish held fast by hooks with tempting baits,
Needing hard hammerblows to break the chains.

Were newspapers the true reflectors of
The people's minds, or true defenders of
Their rights or true reporters of the news,
The world would not be in such mortal risk.
The nuclear engines, too, would not be there
To pose a deadly threat for all the race;
To make the days seem like a nightmare, which
Would be dissolved, as soon as one awakes,
From what is not a normal state of mind
Of homo sapiens, whose instinctive love
Of life kept him alive and kicking through
The rigor of the long glacial age;
But now unhinged by genial luxury
Is bent on self-destruction on the ground
That earth cannot provide sufficient room
For two ascendant states to live in peace,
So either one or both of them must end.

The media, in the relentless grip
Of owners who have their own ends to serve,
Can only act as they are bid to do.
So e'en with such a mortal threat in front
They play it down, as it is not the wish
Of nuclear powers to enlighten all the world,

And make it share the horrid secret or
Have fuller knowledge of the evils and
Iniquities they would prefer to hide.

They play the monster down as many lack
The imagination to evoke the scenes
Of earth-wide slaughter, ravage and distress,
Worse than the most horrendous scenes of hell,
In which the earth, a raging sea of fire,
Turned into a vast man-made inferno, will
Revolve, disgorging flames on every side:
A weird phenomenon in empty space,
The work of man, a new-born, pampered child,
Now lost to sense and shame to this degree,
That, as if drunk, he fails to realize
There is a Power protecting earthly life,
Which has kept her alive since she was born
Billions of years ago, and shall preserve
Her safely, e'en despite the mad designs
Of power-intoxicated men, in a way
That shall put them to grievous loss and shame.

But it is useless to discuss this point,
For God has no share in their thinking on
The world, no part in what they do or say,
No hand, at all, in their affairs, and so
They have no time for topics of this kind;
As sitting on their chairs, absorbed in work,
They snap their orders or dictate their notes
Amid the din of ceaseless telephone calls,

And bustling helpers, running in and out,
Intensely busy at a feverish pitch
Which is unwholesome for the evolving brain;
And, hence, it is no wonder that in this
Excitement they omit to give due thought
To that on which their own existence rests.

We pay a high price for our lack of faith
In Godhead and religion, as that draws
The soul more deeply in the whirl of life,
Where lacking the serenity it needs
To find its bearings in a giddy world,
We fail to see the shadow on our minds
By shutting out the light that shows the stain.

This is the reason why a subject so
Exceedingly important for us all,
For our survival, happiness and peace,
Important as our very life itself,
Important as our breath and far more dear
Than all the dearest objects that we have,
Should be so miserly dealt with by them,
As if it is no more important than
A common topic of which dozens are
To be assigned a place in daily news.

This shows they have not yet awakened to
What nature wishes them to awake at once,
That of the most accomplished brains on earth
A massive part is edged towards decline,

With blunted instinct for survival and
Hence, cannot well assess the importance of
This most momentous of all topics which
Demand attention at this time, the most
Urgent of all the problems that mankind
Will e'er have to resolve in all her life.

Hence they cannot assess the damage done
By their omission to make nuclear arms
A subject most extensively discussed,
Without remission each and every day,
Above one's own opinions, options, views,
Objectives, interests or policy,
And all whate'er conspires to bar the way
To giving full attention to this theme,
So that, in case the dreaded moment comes,
Their conscience does not prick them for the lapse.

They owe a solemn duty to their lands
As also to the world to act, in truth,
As watchdogs to expose dishonesty,
Corruption, laxity and other faults
Of those in power and e'en the common fry,
To save society from grievous harm.
But are these missiles blessings raining down
From heaven, which must be locked up in a chest,
And not exposed in full before the eyes
Of all to know how they affect their lives?
Or are they laurel crowns that should adorn
The most progressive nations of our time,
So that they must be sweetly talked about

And gingerly touched by the media,
To avoid outcry and protests from all lands
When they depict these Monsters in the nude.

Further additions to the nuclear stock,
After what has already been amassed,
Sufficient to wipe off all traces of man
From earth, cannot continue for all time.
There must a state of saturation come,
Beyond which it would be sheer lunacy
To make additions, at enormous cost,
Only to make the situation worse
And drive the opponent, when he perceives
That he cannot maintain the dizzy pace,
In desperation to resort to what
Increase in armament is aimed to check;
Namely to find a cause to start the war,
Dashing one's hopes to avoid it to the ground.

No expert, specialist, adviser or
Commander, head of state or minister
Can e'er be sure what form the war would take,
From what place and on what day it would start,
And what will serve as the igniting spark
That would enwrap the earth with raging fire,
What incident, event or random chance;
What pressure, what ambition or what state
Of madness or frustration or despair
Would cause unhingement of a leading brain
To plunge mankind into the depths of hell;
Or what course would the nuclear battles take,

Which towns would be destroyed, which cities burnt,
Who would win or lose in the bloody fray,
Or no survivors would be left at all.

There is no answer to these vital points
Either from Russia or the watchful West,
Nor anyone upon the face of earth
Can answer them or at the answer guess,
Nor are the populations in the two
Unanimous in their approach to war,
Nor is the great majority inclined
Towards aggression or dispute or fight,
Unless excited violently by
Some injury or a malicious act,
Done by the other side, or when aroused
To furious ire with propaganda tricks
Resorted to by their own leading lights
To inflame the nation so that it may rise
With one voice to condemn and fight the foe,
Never suspecting it is made a tool
By but a fragment they invest with power
To hold their lives in their uncertain hands.

If multitudes in Russia or the West
Were taken into confidence by those
In power and honestly informed about
Their plans, their hopes and fears, and now the chance
Of nuclear battles and the aftermath,
If e'en a tithe of the stockpiles is used;
One can assert with confidence, not e'en

Five percent of the nation would agree.
They would not, either in the Western states
Or Russia, say "yes" to a holocaust.
No man alive, except the insane and warped,
Would give his sanction to a Doomsday kill.

But common folk shall be the luckless prey
To pay for top decisions with their lives.
The best protected and the most secure
Would be the highest few who opt for war,
Against the practice followed in the past
When kings and generals took part in the fight—
The moral duty of those who decide
Upon this course, the natural response
From those who would initiate a line
Of action, viz. courageously to lead
The nation in the step they have advised,
To work like other folk, unsheltered from
The blasts, exposed to all the hazards faced
In war, as was invariably done
On bloody battlefields by mighty kings,
Potentates and commanders in the past.
It was a mark of valor, courage, grit,
Which e'er endeared the Monarch to the crowds
And soldiery—a healthy, natural
And moral pattern of behavior which
Most nations have abandoned. For today
There are no longer healthy battles fought,
But only genocidal total wars—
A ghastly symptom of incipient

Distortion of the human intellect,
Which, if not cured at once, shall end the race.

The sudden turn which war took in the last
Less than one hundred years, in Europe first,
Discarding the time-honored practice of
A face-to-face attack, decided by
Superior courage, weapons, numbers, grit,
Resources, skill, endurance, wit, which had,
At last, the mark of strength and manliness
In those we scornfully call barbarians,
Compared to our high state of culture, wealth
And polish, ne'er awakening to the truth
That we descend below ferocious beasts,
Below the darkest savage of the past,
Below the most depraved of prison-birds,
Below the foul embodiment of sin—
The Devil with all his obnoxious tribe—
When guarded by impregnable defense
We let fly, from a distance, at thick crowds
Of simple folk who never did us harm,
And kill, without compunction, all of them,
As we would do a crowd of nasty flies,
A horrid down-trend of the human mind,
Neglected by the erudite too long;
Of which they should have taken note in time.
But it remained unnoticed, as the learned
Lack in transcendent knowledge of the mind.

We should know that a soft, luxurious life
Is fatal for man's still-expanding mind,

As it creates a poison which infects
The changing nervous structure of the brain—
The reason why patrician nobles fell.
A hot, euphoric life-style swiftly acts
Like deadly poison on the human frame,
Erodes its vigor and depletes its strength,
Distorts and stunts the brain, kills manly traits
Essential, with intelligence and skill,
For healthy, human personalities,
Leaving behind a softened, spineless mass,
Astute and clever, but infirm and lax,
Sensuous, irresolute and indolent,
Like to the fleshpots and voluptuaries,
The last successors of dynastic kings,
Whose orgies fill the pages of history.

This fatal venom, spreading unrestrained
To all the toiling legions of the earth,
Would soon produce degenerate racial types,
Obsessed with animal concerns alone,
Of wealth, possession, status, color, caste,
Of pleasure, women, dresses, food and drink,
Profession, business, office, hobby, craft,
With no thought to their faith or principles,
To their eternal soul or after-life,
To honor, duty, self-respect or truth,
Religious striving, meditation or
Some form of worship, prayer or discourse,
To rise above the carnal and remind
Oneself, at times, that his immortal soul

Belongs to purer, nobler planes of being;
And, sans this feeling, he is no more than
A deft, intelligent, pleasure-seeking brute,
Who has no right to say, "I have a soul!"

The scholars, rulers and all those concerned
With social problems now, whose mature views
In books and journals are relayed with pride
By media all o'er the busy world,
And heard attentively by listening crowds,
But seldom make this topic, too, a theme
In their discussions or discourses, which
Has been a serious lapse, so serious that
A rigid fast is now the only cure.

That is the reason why subconscious urges
In fanatics, destined to act this part,
Are madly after a suicidal war,
To cause a state of horror, suffering, pain,
A period so full of adversities,
Displacement, famine, want, disease and death,
Affliction, sorrow, strain, distress and loss,
That sheer exhaustion, dearth and agony
Would cause a sudden halt to this abuse,
And such revulsion 'gainst this way of life,
And those who favored and commended it,
That, for long centuries, the chastened race
Would shrink away from the licentious path,
As from a viper, and recall with shame
The pompous front-men who thought they were wise

O, self-applauding, Sir, with countless faults
In our own selves, we haste to lay the blame
For them, not on ourselves, but Lucifer,
Thus making him a scapegoat for our sins.

Much of the current thinking of the race,
Imparted to the crowds by leading minds,
Is colored by a hardly noticed taint
Of mental aberration, covered by
A thin veneer of soft urbanity
And culture, which is washed off all at once
When hate or anger takes possession of
A nation or a group, resulting in
Barbarities which put wild beasts to shame.
The race has clearly lost her bearings in
The yet uncharted province of her mind.
To bring her back to sanity and sense—
A hopeless task for scholars to perform—
A sour dose of affliction is the need,
As otherwise the smart, agnostic rank
Of highest intellects and talent sees
No sign of Godhead anywhere and, proud
Of their tellurian triumphs, feel assured
That what they do is right and that no power
In heaven, if it exists, can dare undo
What they have done or keep from acting thus—
A morbid attitude of mind against
The Law Divine that Man must mold his life
In the religion-born idea of God,
And live in full surrender to His Will,
The safest pathway for the evolving brain.

Instead of solving burning problems soon,
To make sure that the race abides in peace,
The learned of the day amuse themselves
By taking up droll studies that could wait.
They squander millions in surveying far
And wide for traces of a similar freak,
The same unique organic structure wrought
By the same elements, adorning yet
Another planet in the Universe,
With whom they could communicate and then,
O, joy, share with them their terrestrial life,
Their thoughts and dreams, their sorrows and delights
To be co-sharers in what they have learnt
On their own planet: How to make one's life
More happy and euphoric, how to win
More secrets of dynamic forces and
How to become the Sovereign Lord of all.

O, these vain dreams and wishful fantasies
Of this deluded creature who, when in
His prime behaves and acts as if the world
Belongs to him alone, disdainful of
The poor and low, but when bowed down with age
And illness, looks with envy at the youth
And vigor of the very creatures whom
In his heyday of life he had despised.
On both occasions wholly in the dark:
What hid mechanism wrought in him the change?

What made him think so highly of himself,
As if intoxicated all the time;

But, when beleaguered by advancing age,
What made the lion shaky, like a lamb,
Looking pathetic, when, with anxious eyes,
He furtively regards a rushing crowd,
Uncertain how to make his way across,
Where he had buoyantly pushed through when young

A poor sleepwalker who knows not himself,
Nor whence he came nor where he has to go,
Lost in the labyrinth of phantom worlds,
Of nebulae and galaxies, who lives
Transfixed with wonder at the sights he sees,
Not knowing in the least wherefor and how,
Until with anguish at the heart he leaves
The prison still awareless why he came?

This is the sorry end of mortal life,
Spent in observing from the birth to death
An endless Drama filled with woeful and
Delightful, banal and exciting scenes—
In which the actor never knows his role,
Nor who allotted him the special part,
Nor how he would perform it, well or ill,
Nor who would judge the merit of his acts,
Nor how this last adjudgment would result,
In laurels or the lash, in heaven or hell,
Or in succeeding visits to the earth—
A host of riddles sitting heavy on
The minds of countless more discerning folk,
To find an answer well before the end.

The outcome of our lack of study in
The sacred lore of all religions and
Investigation of the claims made by
The Founders, that their Message was revealed,
Is obvious in the present crisis which,
Despite all efforts, nations fail to solve;
Which makes a large part of the race to live
In terror and suspense about the end.
This is the fruit of our revolt against
The law, the harvest of our disbelief
In our divine existence as a Soul,
Unbound and everlasting, free from death,
Disease, decay and age, the timeless drop
From Life's Eternal Deep, which we are born
To plumb, to win again the Kingdom lost—
The crowning Glory of embodied life,
The Prize Supreme for all the travail borne;
The Answer to the Eternal Mystery
Of Life, a hint about the glorious fate
Of mankind, when devout and self-subdued
She works hard for the Vision of her Self.

But save a few innately favored souls,
Who are pursuing those sublime ideals,
To live a life of service, joy and peace,
Denied to high and mighty of the day,
By far the greater part devote their time
And talent purely for material ends,
And most of them, all their life, only move
Inside this soul-neglecting, earthly groove.

This all-consuming passion for the world
And its allurements, when beyond confines,
Creates perverse reactions in the mind,
In morbid thought, desire and appetite,
Or in abnormal working of the brain,
Dispersed attention, wit, activity,
And disproportionate instinctive traits—
The ominous forerunners of mental fault,
Erratic conduct and behavior,
In milder forms which are so rife today.

What answer have we to this riddle: Why
There is such lack of saving wisdom on
The part of leaders and such apathy
On that of people of the foremost lands
Of learning and abundance, which makes them
Oblivious to the grim position that
They, as a nation, are as good as dead,
If they do not devise new ways to live,
In lasting peace, with friends and foes alike,
In future years, for e'en a single clash,
With nuclear arms, would cause such havoc that
No country will survive intact and whole,
Or hope to be 'gain what she was before!

If e'en now they persist in holding fast
To drastic ways of settling disputes,
With gun and cannon, or resort to war
To gain preeminence, resources, wealth
Or territory, it means that they are not

Alert enough to draw their minds out of
A most pernicious, unadoptable rut,
Like moths reluctant to give up a flame
Until, one moment, it their life destroys.

Ah, what an irony that those who wrought
So great and wonderful a change in all
The spheres of knowledge, science, arts and crafts
All over, should now by a sad decree
Of Fate, refuse to make a similar change
In their attempts to solve the problem of
Pacific coexistence, in the years
To come, for all the nations on the earth.
There can be and must be far better ways
Of intercourse between the nations than
The ones they follow to invite at once
A grim catastrophe for all the race.

What heavy stupor has benumbed the will
To live in e'en the keenest intellects,
And what inertness has gripped, like a vice,
The brilliant minds of all the leading lights
Of mankind, so that they are standing limp
And motionless before a gathering storm
Of fire and brimstone, which would not permit
A single nation to escape unhurt?
Why, like a herd of cattle, are the crowds
Looking at one another for a cue
About their own behavior, knowing that
There shortly might occur stampedes so mad
That millions would be trampled under feet?

Why, as if paralysed, there is no stir
Among the neutral nations to decry
This new potential threat to their own life,
Their assets, children, consorts, kith and kin;
To what is basic for survival and
To health and happiness, to joy and peace,
To what makes earthly life so dear to us.

For the historians of our hectic age
The most portentous of the glaring signs
They would observe, foredooming all the race
To death, unthinkable horror and distress,
Is this unnatural inertia
And apathy towards a danger so
Extreme and imminent that only those
Under hypnosis or an opiate,
Or with a rare narcosis of the brain,
Would show, when fronted by a mortal threat,
When circled by a pack of hungry wolves,
Man-eating tigers or ferocious lions,
Or e'en more savage and inhuman bands
Of gangsters, terrorists or vile dacoits.

This numbness of the mind towards a fate
So grim and hideous, so immediate,
Denotes a mental torpor so acute
It gives the impression that we dumbly wait
For Nemesis to do her ghastly work.

'Tis inconceivable that a sturdy race
That has survived the tempests and the storms,

Misfortunes and reverses in the past,
For vast aeonian spans of time, should be
So dead towards her own existence now
That e'en the fear of her extinction in
The years to come is not strong enough
To rouse her from the stupor which, it seems,
Has paralysed the basic instinct for
Self-preservation, planted deep within,
In every healthy form of life on earth,
Which when inert denotes insanity,
With self-destructive trends, or symptoms of
Inertness of the brain preceding death.

THE DESTRUCTION OF SODOM
Genesis xviii, xix.

The whole horizon is ablaze; the walls of the doomed city are fairly torn
asunder by the furious sweep of the flames, while the stifling smoke rolls
upward in tumultous volumes, filling all the upper sky with blackness,
and spreading gloom over the earth.

CHAPTER X

THE ONLY SURE AND HONORABLE WAY OUT

How would the law adjudge the acts of one
Who proves a traitor to his motherland,
Deceives the nation, sells her to a foe,
Imposes on her and betrays her trust,
Tells vital secrets to her enemies,
Dishonors her in the eyes of the world,
And by these actions does her grievous harm.
He braves the anger of his country-folk,
Draws on himself their insults and abuse,
Disgrace and condemnation for his crime;
Aware they would despise and hate his name,
And, if in their grip, would demand his life,
To avenge the serious wrong he did to them.
He knows all this when he commits the sin,
Driven to it by burning thirst for gold,
Or high position or possession or
His passion for a charmer whom he loves,
Who lured him from his nation and his home
And made him face the tempest for her sake.

If we conceive Faith as our native land,
The soil on which we were brought up and bred,
With God as Sovereign Ruler, Heaven as home,
And heavenly beings as compatriots,
Which is the true position, if we trust
The gospels of our creed, declaring that
We are the children of a heavenly Sire,
With angels, cherubim and devas as
Our close companions, dwellers on the land
To which, in solemn truth, we all belong—
The land of seraphs and immortal orbs
Of life-divine, who drest in clay descend
To earth to play their parts, allotted by
The Sire, in keeping with Celestial Laws,
Beyond our ken, as girt by walls of clay,
We lose touch with the customs of our land
And need, to win back our divine estate,
Continued effort to unearth the Key.

O, ye Believers in Religion and
The Truths which it upholds for common good,
How can we justify our lack of faith
When we shut from the mind our pure descent,
Our high position as Empyrean-born,
Our tall imperial stature as a Soul,
Above the good and evil of the earth,
Above its opulence and poverty,
Above its storm and stress, dispute and strife,
Above its squalor, dirt, refuse and filth,
Above all that disturbs us in the least,

Or acts against our native state of bliss
That reigns supreme in our celestial home,
Above the din and noise, disease and pain,
Despair and hope, distress and fleeting joy,
Which make up, for a while, our worldly life?

Why have we given up this gold to waste
The Time allowed to us by waiting death,
In heaping litter and in hoarding trash,
Which, when beyond our need, are valueless
And only satisfy a morbid itch
For show and grandeur, boundless power or wealth,
Or mad desire for all-devouring love,
Which all end in frustration or remorse
Or vain regrets, when with decaying health
And bent with age, we ponder o'er the past?

There can be no two views about the fact
That we cannot be loyal to our faith,
If we discredit its accepted truths,
Or fail to act upon the injunctions laid
To discipline our lives in keeping with
Its tenets and beliefs held all along.
We must behave, if loyal to our creed,
Which tells us that we have a deathless soul,
In ways which do not savor of pretense
Of guile or false belief to save our face,
And must work diligently all our life
To gain the Kingdom of Heaven, Nirvana
Or Paradise or Brahman, as the Peak

For which we have to strive, with all our strength,
And how: This too is clearly underlined
In Sermon on the Mount, Commandments Ten,
The Gita, Dhammapada or Quran
And scriptures of the other holy faiths.

How can we class a mortal who is loud
In his avowal of a holy faith,
But does the opposite of what she says,
Calls God his Father or Creator or
By what-so-e'er relationship he likes;
But by his acts belies the love professed;
Accepts that his soul is immortal and
That Gospels hold inspired commands of God,
Or of His incarnation, or of One
Among the highest of enlightened Souls,
Or of a Prophet with a Message from
The Lord to show the right way to the fold;
But far from acting on the precepts taught
Does the reverse, obeys the cannons laid
By breaking each and every one of them,
Invokes the Grace of God for help in need,
And then repays it with ingratitude;
Except in lip-deep worship, prayer, rites,
Ignores the Gospels as if of no worth;
A fibster, outwardly who owns a creed
With lips, but soon disowns it with his deeds;
A crime worse than unmasked apostasy.

How far do we obey the tenets of
Our faith, how far act on the word of God,
Can be assessed by our aversion to
A simple, humble life of peace and truth,
Compassion, love for neighbor, charity,
Subdued ambition, passion, lust, desire,
Downgraded anger, hate and violence:
A life attuned to God and His image pure
Of what is good and noble in the world.
But what will we find, if we try to probe
How far our life is modelled on our Faith;
How far we reach the ideals carved by her,
How far we carry out the Will of God?
If we are lax, what do we merit for
Our gross intransigence 'gainst the laws,
Against what is ambrosia for the soul,
Whom we drag in the mud of our desire;
Against what can attest our love of God
Against all that we must uphold as right
If we admit we have a soul to save,
To prove we are above unthinking beasts,
And have a Crown of wit upon our head?

But if we fail in this emergent task
And act contrarily, then are we not
As good as traitors to our native soil,
Seduced from duty by the very same
Alluring chattels which entice one who
Betrays his country for some tempting bait?
Is it surprising then that Man is faced
With a threat to his whole community?

The menace, too, does not descend from heaven
But is our own creation, for it is
Born of our own intelligence and wit,
Which are the prompters, too, of our revolt.
And so our treason 'gainst our native land
In dire calamity might soon recoil.
'Tis our superb intelligence that won
For us the richest empire on the earth,
But now an outlaw for her grave defiance
Is waiting for the Rod to set her right.

Do you think in the preparations made
For war the Powers-that-be can have no hand,
And that the nuclear weapons, forged by us,
Have not their concurrence and active help?
Have you e'er pondered o'er the issue that
The Omnipresent and Omniscient God
Can ne'er be ignorant of what we do,
Nor can we act against His edicts nor
Can aught materialize against His Will?

So, if a true believer, one cannot
Refuse to own that we are face to face
With that phenomenon which ancients called
The "Wrath of Heaven," descending on the earth,
To put insurgent Man back on the Path.
And so the weapons, piled up fast, provide
The scourge, devised by human wit, to whip
Herself to sanity, with awful pain,
Out of her drunken state of arrogance.

The plea that progress in technology
Confers on those who can prepare the stuff
The right to use atomic armaments
Is as untenable as the logic that
One who invents a new machine-gun can
Employ it lawfully in a roadside fray
To win more honor from his neighbors, or
A larger portion from the market stock,
Or a predominant position in
The neighborhood with greater right to grab
Whate'er he chooses for the reason that
He is more powerful, richer, more advanced,
And has a new machine-gun in his hand!

Or if a man discovers a new way
Of dalliance with women he should be
Allowed to show his skill in public parks
Before the eager eyes of hungry crowds!
Or let a student who invents a bomb
Which, using only air, can kill a crowd,
Can deploy the new device, when in class,
To cow down teachers, frighten other boys,
Or rob the school of books and magazines,
And, when restrained, explode in self-defense
To blast the offending kids, as their restraint
Would mean infringement of his right to do
Whate'er he likes with this new wonder of
His more enhanced skill in technology.

The truth is that a vile, infernal stuff,
Prepared in secrecy by clever brains,

By wrongly using their great intellects,
Howe'er high in repute they might have been,
Howe'er high their attainments and their skill,
To be used by their nation which, without
Regard to principles of justice, truth
And fair play, laws of ethics, human rights,
Divine Commandments and the rules of war,
Employed it for revenge on innocents.
To exact the penalty imposed for such
A wild defiance of Celestial Law,
The stuff—assuming now the awful form
Of an infernal Monster—is about
To pounce upon the guilty intellect,
And hovers close to every spot on earth
The ends of heavenly justice soon to serve.
A Dragon reared up by man with his wit,
To inflict due punishment for guilty acts
Of his own and to learn a lesson which
He shall recall with awe for centuries.

The wonder is how all the world is dead
To so gross a denial of the rights
Of other nations, threatened by the blasts,
Though not a party to the deadly feud,
Who run the risk of radiation, death,
Pollution, famine, dearth, disruption, loss
And e'en a direct hit with missiles, when
The war is at its height, and palsied hands,
Inert with horror at the ghastly sights,
Mis-aim the monsters to unchosen sites.

Who will then pay the damage done as none
Out of the parties may survive the clash,
Or be in a position to make good
The loss inflicted on a neutral land,
Which is inevitable in a war
With nuclear engines of the latest type?

This raises issues how on moral grounds,
And how, while advocating human rights,
A nation can deploy a weapon so
Uncertain and unmanageable that
It can cause grievous harm to distant soils,
And wreck and ruin them beyond repair,
Can damage and disrupt contiguous lands,
In no respect connected with the war,
With fallout and contamination of
The native elements essential for
The existence and survival of their life?

How can we justify a weapon which
Can prove as lethal for non-combatants
As for belligerents? Where is the law
Or e'en convention which permits a state,
Wittingly or unwittingly, to blast
A neutral land, with irreparable loss
Of life and property to its unarmed
And guiltless folk? How can a foul device,
That has this possibility, be used
By nations proud of their traditions for
Uprightness, freedom, justice, rule of law,

And human feeling shown for all the race?
How can they reconcile the two, O God?
How can they reconcile their word and deed?

It is beyond the slightest shade of doubt
That, judged by any standard, e'en of war,
The use of nuclear weapons is a crime
Against both man and God, and all upheld
As Right by law and world religions both.
No arguments or logic can defend
What will be undefendable to the end.
'Tis but a waste of time and energy
To whitewash what is but a heinous crime.
How odd that this egregious sin is made
A subject of debate, when it would meet
Only contempt and condemnation from
The law-abiding nine-tenths of the race.

The nuclear nations know it too well that
Their lives will be in gravest danger, when
Atomic weapons are employed, and hence
Those well informed about this menace try
Their best to end the overhanging threat,
To save their own dear lives, well knowing that
They may cause e'en more damage to their land
Than to that of the distant enemy,
For no one can predict whose aim will be
More true, or favored more by chance, to hit
The most strategic sites on either side.

We know these foul contraptions have not been
Accepted e'en by all the people of
The nuclear nations, and but one exchange
Of fire might cause upheavals that may force
The ones in power to quit or end the war.
Those who are counting on the nuclear arm
For their ascendancy, survival or
Subdual of the foe live in the land
Of dreamers, and will be the first to reap
The fruit of their revolt against the Law,
By paying forfeit with their robes and gowns;
For such a murderous frenzy will soon grip
The crowds that they will stop at nothing, and
May rise in mad rebellion 'gainst the few
In power who will be out-and-out for war
To end at once the diabolic fray.

How does the conscience of the leading ranks
Of these ascendant lands remain unpricked,
When they know that their own compatriots
Live with a dread sword hanging o'er their heads;
That pregnant mothers, crowing babies and
The toiling crowds of simple, honest folk,
Who bide contented with the tithe they have,
Delighted to be moving and alive,
Will all be instantly hurled into hell,
For no fault on their part, no sin, no wrong,
No action done to merit such an end,
Save that of cheering loud the ruling teams
Whene'er they chanced to pass their way or, when

They saw them in a gala function held
To listen to the words they had to say—
Without least knowledge of their hid designs
Or actions or what they intend to do—
A state of trust unparalleled on earth,
But often from one side alone, returned
But seldom by the other and, sometimes,
Repaid with treachery by those adored?

If all the world upholds this kind of war,
This murder from a distance of the folk
Of hostile lands, in millions at a time,
Unarmed, defenseless women, children, men—
That does not mean 'tis not a heinous crime.

If all the world upholds a way of life
Which contravenes the gospels of a faith,
And acts conversely to the precepts taught,
Or revels in defying all the rules,
That does not mean adherents of that creed
Are right in their behavior, in the least,
Or true to their profession or belief.

If all the world upholds ideals which
Confer equality on one and all,
With liberty and brotherhood to add,
And then to enforce these high ideals puts
To sword and into concentration camps,
For grinding labor with frostbitten hands,
Millions of victims in dark secrecy,

It does not mean that what is done is right
And that the principles professed are sound.

This is what ails the clever mind today,
'Tis dead to its transgressions all the time;
It ne'er perceives the ugly, darker side
Of its behavior or its thought and act,
And, as one pets a sweetheart, hugs its faults,
Condones its errors, justifies mistakes,
Excuses misdemeanors, waives off sins,
By self-deceit keeps merry all the time,
Dwells on but its good traits, ignores the bad,
Which, when remembered, might its conscience prick,
And thus, oblivious to its own defects,
Which one must keep before one's eye to mend,
With slow erosion of the moral side,
Has made embellished lie a passable norm
Of man's behavior in his business deals—
A practice which, condemned by every faith,
Is honey to sophisticated minds.

The outcome is that of the leading brains
The bulk delights in what it thinks or does
And often views an action, e'en if wrong,
In the light of its broader interests;
Or of the high position which it holds,
Judging them not by the criteria laid,
Nor by some standard fixed for what is right,
But by its interests, objectives, aims,
Or nature of the expediency—

An egotistic and narcissistic mind,
Which firm believes 'tis always in the right
And salves its conscience with the logic that
This was the only course it could pursue;
In that position all would do the same;
That was how it could best its country serve,
Its firm or office or its interest,
Casting morality in diverse molds,
Like wax, to make it suit its ends and aims.

Since moral values are essential for
Mankind's survival in the atomic age,
It would be virtual suicide to break
The wall that stands between us and sure death.
'Tis for this reason that the actions done
By leading minds in all academies,
In trade, in politics, professions, arts
Or in the media—the leading wit
And skill in every sphere of human life—
Unless restrained by strict adherence to
The Moral Laws would jeopardise the race.
The present crisis is a warning sign
From heaven, reminding us to change our ways;
But since we are bedazzled by the glow
Of our achievements in the earthly fields,
There is a common error that we can
Defy the moral laws that rule our lives,
A fatal blunder at the very base
Of dangers which now stare us in the face.

A full-blown nuclear war is suicide,
A mad itch for self-immolation done
To meet some foul distemper of the mind,
For sanity can ne'er become so mad
To walk into the jaws of death at choice.
Those who display a lack of sense to see
The present hideous conflict in this light
Betray a deadness of the instinct for
Self-preservation, the primordial urge
On which survival of the race depends.

A half-way nuclear war is out of count,
For once the Demon of Hate is at large,
And the exchange of nuclear missiles starts,
With capitals as the first targets hit,
Who will retain the sanity of mind
To call a halt to the exploding bombs!
For there will not be one but many states
Involved in this infernal give and take,
With wounded, dying and dead everywhere,
The country in a shambles, transport and
Communication wrecked, the leaders out
Of wits, a thousand problems on their mind;
The people in the grip of mortal fear,
Running in panic, dead to everything
Save how to flee from the pursuing flames;
A wild stampede, more than frantic rush,
In which the weaker would be crushed to death;
Who will maintain his balance, keep his wits
In these macabre, mind-unhinging scenes,

Unfolding with the speed of lightning and
Beyond the power of man to handle now?

Those who complacently talk of this threat
Which can make earth a fuming hell in space,
While lolling in their chairs, with pen in hand,
Smoking, as if they are the lords of earth,
Looking so calm and undisturbed, the while
They speak on this unspeakable curse of war,
Treating atomic fights, too, as routine,
Howe'er accomplished, are a hopeless prey
To that abnormal state of intellect,
Which barren of compassion and the power
To place herself in the shoes of the crowds
That will fall victims to the awful blasts,
And form the objects of those grisly scenes,
They, like the color-blind who have no sense
Of color, fail to assess the pain involved—
A common failing of conceited minds,
Which all their life think only of themselves,
Against injunctions laid by every faith
To think of others in one's prayers and
To exercise compassion off and on.

For sans this love of neighbor and the thought
Of poor and helpless in one's daily life,
The mind becomes too self-indulgent to
Think kindly and humanely of the world—
The type of mind neglect of faith has bred.

The mighty heads of states, on whom devolves
The great responsibility of our time
To avert the threatened holocaust, should not
Bend low to listen to the phobic lot,
Who ne'er can taste the bitterness of that
Which they propose unless themselves hit hard.
The only potent method to resolve
This hard dilemma is to moderate
The heat, stop adding fuel to the fire,
And slowly bring to a halt the weapon race,
Convene effective meetings of the states
Which stand up stoutly for a peaceful world,
Ban weapon sales to needy lands for gain,
For you thus arm yourself potential foes,
Nor e'en supply them free to your allies;
Reduce production of this ware until
The curse of war is lifted from the earth.

Key up the U.N.O. to push this cause,
Alert the people of all lands and climes
About the dangers of a nuclear war,
In duty bound, as you first should have done
Before embarking on this fatal course.
Enlist their full support in this campaign,
Their cry will be resistless and shall win
E'en in the lands where their voice is suppressed.
Begin discussions with the foe to evolve
A formula for coexistence in
A climate of peace, friendship, love and trust,
And draw up soon a mutual agreement,

With fullest safeguards set for either side,
Each bound to observe for e'er the solemn pact,
Each bound to honor and respect those who
Are parties to this holy covenant.

This is the only dignified way out,
The only sure and honorable course,
Which, with pure efforts and the Grace of God,
Can grant humanity a further lease
Of life to win the glorious prize ordained
To crown her hard millennial toil on earth.
Do not forget when in fear of this war
That Hope is ne'er away from human hearts,
And blank despair is ne'er the only course
For those beleaguered by an adverse Fate,
As Grace of God is always near at hand
To fill the darkest day with bright sunshine.

End

THE ASCENSION
Mark xvi. 19; Luke xxiv, 50–53; Acts i. 9–12

"And it came to pass, while he blessed them, he was parted from them, and carried up into heaven."

GLOSSARY

aberrated—ABERRANT: straying from the right or normal way; deviating from the usual or natural type.

adept (n.)—(from "adeptus," an alchemist who has attained the knowledge of how to "change base metals into gold," i.e., to transmute sexual energy for illumination; a highly skilled or well-trained individual; one who has attained to a higher than normal level of evolution and has knowledge from a superphysical source and/or control of the unseen forces of nature (e.g., psychical powers).

abject—SERVILE, SPIRITLESS: utterly hopeless.

abstemious—sparingly used or indulged in.

affray—FRAY, BRAWL, FIGHT.

alchemic—marked by a supposedly great or magic power of transmutation; [alchemy: a doctrine concerning the regeneration and perfection of man (i.e., the process of individuation and evolution), concealed under a terminology of chemical terms, allegories, fables, and symbols]; see ADEPT.

anchorite—one who renounces the world to live in seclusion, usually for religious reasons: HERMIT, RECLUSE.

anomalous—deviating from a general rule, method, or analogy: ABNORMAL: being out of keeping with accepted notions of fitness or order; IRREGULAR

apostasy—abandonment of a previous loyalty: DEFECTION.

artifice—an artful trick; false or insincere behavior; CONTRIVANCE.

ascetic (n.)—one who practices strict self-denial (e.g., celibacy, fasting, and self-mortification) and who devotes himself to a life of solitude and contemplation, as a measure of personal and especially spiritual discipline.

aspersion—a critical and usually censorious remark; adverse criticism.

assuage—to put an end to by satisfying: APPEASE, QUENCH; RELIEVE.

astral—of or relating to the stars; consisting of, belonging to, or being a supersensible substance supposed to be next above the tangible world in refinement.

astral forces—superphysical forces.

bantling—a very young child.

beatitude—a state of utmost bliss.

belie—to prove false; to run counter to: CONTRADICT; MISREPRESENT.

benighted—existing in a state of intellectual, moral, or social darkness: UNENLIGHTENED.

boons—BENEFITS, FAVORS: especially ones that are given in answer to a request; BLESSINGS.

bourne—BOUNDARY, LIMIT; GOAL, DESTINATION.

Brahman—the ultimate ground of all being in Hinduism; GOD, COSMIC CONSCIOUSNESS.

Brahmin—a Hindu of the highest caste traditionally assigned to the priesthood, having as his chief duty the study and teaching of the Vedas and the performance of religious ceremonies.

buffet (n.)—a blow (of great force).

burnished—made shiny or lustrous, especially by rubbing: POLISHED.

carnage—great and bloody slaughter: MASSACRE.

carnal—relating to or given to crude bodily pleasures and appetites; marked by sexuality; WORLDLY; FLESHLY.

cats'-paws—one used by another as a tool: DUPE (from the fable of the monkey that used a cat's paw to draw chestnuts from the fire).

chela—a disciple or follower.

cherubim—biblical figures frequently represented as composite beings with large wings, human heads, and animal bodies and regarded as guardians of a sacred place and as servants of God; an order of angels ordinarily symbolizing divine wisdom or justice.

chimera—an illusion or fabrication of the mind, especially an unrealizable dream.

citrine—resembling a citron or Lemon, especially in color.

compunction—anxiety arising from awareness of guilt; distress of mind over an anticipated action or result; a twinge of misgiving; PENITENCE, QUALM.

condone—to pardon or overlook voluntarily, especially to treat as if trivial, harmless, or of no importance; EXCUSE.

confreres—COLLEAGUES, COMRADES.

contiguous—ADJACENT.

contravene—to go or act contrary to; CONTRADICT; DENY; VIOLATE.

convivial—relating to, occupied with, or fond of feasting, drinking, and good company.

covenant—a usually formal, solemn, and binding agreement: COMPACT.

coxcomb—a conceited foolish person: FOP, FOOL, DUPE.

crass—having such grossness of mind as precludes delicacy and discrimination: INSENSITIVE; STUPID.

credal—pertaining to a set of fundamental beliefs, especially religious belief.

credulity—undue readiness of belief: GULLIBILITY.

cupidity—strong desire: LUST; inordinate desire for wealth: AVARICE, GREED.

cur—a mongrel or a mutt.

dacoit—one of a class of criminals in India and Burma who rob and murder in roving gangs.

dearth—scarcity that makes dear, specifically: FAMINE; an inadequate supply: LACK.

debacle—a great disaster; a complete failure: FIASCO.

decimate—to select by lot and kill

every tenth man of; to destroy a large part of.

decoctions—extracts obtained by boiling.

deign—to condescend reluctantly and with a strong sense of the affront to one's superiority that is involved; to condescend to give or offer; STOOP.

demur—hesitation, usually based on doubt of the acceptability of something offered or proposed; OBJECTION, PROTEST.

demurely—reservedly or modestly but with affectation and pretense.

denizens—INHABITANTS; ones admitted to residence in a foreign country, especially aliens admitted to rights of citizenship; ones that frequent a place.

deva—a divine being or god in Hinduism and Buddhism.

disgorging—VOMITING; discharging violently, confusedly, or as a result of force.

dissension—DISAGREEMENT, especially: partisan and contentious quarreling; DISCORD.

diurnal—DAILY.

dons (n.)—men of elevated rank or station; college or university professors.

eclat—dazzling effect: BRILLIANCE; ostentatious display: PUBLICITY; ACCLAIM, APPLAUSE.

ecstatic trance (mystical ecstasy)—a temporary state of illumination or mystical experience, affecting the intellect and the will with such intensity that the physical powers and external senses are overcome by the vision.

effervescence—a lively bubble or hiss.

effete—no longer fertile; worn out with age; marked by weakness or decadence; OUTMODED.

effluvium—an invisible emanation, especially an offensive exhalation or smell; a by-product, especially in the form of waste.

egotistic—characterized by egotism (an exaggerated sense of self-importance): CONCEITED.

egregious—conspicuously bad: FLAGRANT.

Eldorado—a city or country of fabulous riches held by 16th century explorers to exist in South America; a place of fabulous wealth, abundance, or opportunity.

Elysium—PARADISE.

embellished—DECORATED, ENHANCED; ADORNED.

empyrean (adj.)—of or relating to the empyrean (the highest heaven or heavenly sphere in ancient and medieval cosmology, usually consisting of fire or light; the true and ultimate heavenly paradise); CELESTIAL, SUBLIME.

enfettered—bound in fetters: ENCHAINED.

erstwhile—in the past: FORMERLY.

eschew—to avoid habitually,

especially on moral or practical grounds: SHUN.

evanescent—tending to vanish like vapor: TRANSIENT.

excrescence—an abnormal, excessive, or useless outgrowth.

exhortations—urgent appeals, advice, or warnings.

exigency—a state of affairs requiring immediate aid or action.

expediency—the quality or state of being suited to the end in view; a means of achieving a particular end.

faggots—bundles of sticks.

fanaticism—fanatic (marked by excessive enthusiasm and often intense uncritical devotion) outlook or behavior.

fell (adj.)—FIERCE, CRUEL, TERRIBLE; very destructive or painful: DEADLY.

fleshpots—places of luxurious entertainment.

foment—to promote the growth or development of: ROUSE, INCITE.

forbear—to hold oneself back from, especially with an effort of self-restraint; to hold back: ABSTAIN; to control oneself when provoked: be patient; REFRAIN.

forbode—FORETELL, PORTEND.

foundling—an infant found after its unknown parents have abandoned it.

fray (n.)—BRAWL, FIGHT; DISPUTE.

froth—something unsubstantial or of little value.

genial—favorable to growth or comfort: MILD: GRACIOUS.

giddy—lightheartedly silly: FRIVOLOUS; causing dizziness; DIZZY.

glean—to gather information or other material bit by bit; to pick over in search of relevant material; to find out: LEARN, ASCERTAIN.

Gnosis—KNOWLEDGE, SPIRITUAL TRUTH.

Golconda—(Golconda, India, famous for its diamonds): a rich mine; broadly, a source of great wealth.

guileless—INNOCENT, NAIVE.

Guru—a personal religious teacher and spiritual guide in Hinduism: PRECEPTOR.

hackneyed—lacking in freshness or originality.

heinous—hatefully or shockingly evil: ABOMINABLE; OUTRAGEOUS.

Hermetic Arts—[from Hermes Trismegistus (thrice-great Hermes) Thoth]: relating to or characterized by occultism, alchemy, magic, or whatever is obscure and mysterious; of or relating to the writings or teachings of Thoth, the ancient Egyptian personification of Universal Wisdom, fabled author of a number of mystical, philosophical, and alchemistic writings; teachings which essentially concern self-mastery through the regeneration of the body, the transmutation of the emotions, and the illumination of the mind.

hermit—ANCHORITE,
RECLUSE; specifically a
Christian ascetic living alone
in order to practice religious
exercises.

Hind—India

hoary—impressively or venerably
old: ANCIENT.

holocaust—a sacrifice consumed
by fire; a thorough
destruction, especially by fire.

homage—a ceremony by which a
man acknowledges himself the
vassal of a lord; reverential
regard: DEFERENCE;
HONOR.

Huxley, Thomas H. (1825–1895)—
British biologist and educator
who, in his book, *Man's Place
in Nature* (1863), first
expounded the thesis that
man's closest relatives are the
anthropoid apes, causing much
controversy. Huxley met
Charles Darwin in 1851, and
the two maintained a close
relationship thereafter.

illumination—a transformation of
consciousness, the opening
within of a new channel of
supersensory perception, by
which the deathless and
boundless universe is opened
to the vision of the soul;
a superhuman level of
consciousness in which one
becomes receptive to
Revelation; also known as
union with God; see
MYSTICAL EXPERIENCE.

imp—a small demon: FIEND.

imperious—COMMANDING,
DOMINANT; DOMINEER-
ING; intensely compelling;
MASTERFUL.

inane—EMPTY, INSUBSTAN-
TIAL; lacking significance,
meaning or point: SILLY.

incipient—beginning to come into
being or to become apparent:
COMMENCING.

indolent—slow to develop or heal;
averse to activity, effort, or
movement; LAZY.

inducted—prompted, caused;
INTRODUCED, INITIATED.

inexorable—not to be persuaded
or moved by entreaty:
RELENTLESS; INFLEXIBLE

infernal—of or relating to a nether
world of the dead; of or
relating to hell; HELLISH,
DIABOLICAL; DAMNABLE.

infirm—of poor or deteriorated
vitality; weak of mind, will, or
character: IRRESOLUTE,
VACILLATING; not solid or
stable; WEAK.

inglorious—not glorious: lacking
fame or honor; SHAMEFUL,
DISGRACEFUL;
DEGRADING.

iniquities—gross injustices.

inscrutable—not readily investigated
or interpreted: hard to grasp;
MYSTERIOUS.

insentient—lacking perception,
consciousness, or animation.

insurgent (adj.)—rising in opposition to civil authority or
established leadership:
REBELLIOUS.

intransigence—the quality or
state of being intransigent
(refusing to compromise or
budge from an often extreme

position taken or held:
preserving an immovable
independence of position or
attitude: UNCOMPRO-
MISING).

ire—intense and usually openly
displayed anger.

irresolute—uncertain how to act
or proceed: VACILLATING.

jaundiced—yellowed.

jinn—(jinni) one of a class of
spirits that according to
Muslim demonology inhabit
the earth, assume various
forms, and exercise supernatural power; a supernatural
spirit that often takes human
form and serves his summoner;
said to be of a fiery sub-
tance and in general more
prone to evil.

jocular—given to jesting: habitually jolly and high spirited;
PLAYFUL.

jot—the least bit: IOTA.

kith—familiar friends, neighbors,
or relatives.

lacunae—blank spaces or missing
parts: GAPS.

Lama—a Lamaist monk or priest
(Lamaism: the Mahayana
Buddhism of Tibet and
Mongolia marked by tantric
and shamanistic ritual and a
dominant monastic hierarchy
headed by the Dalai Lama).

lax—deficient in firmness:
LOOSE, NEGLIGENT.

lethargy—abnormal drowsiness;
the quality or state of being
lazy or indifferent.

macabre—having death as a
subject; dwelling on the

gruesome; tending to produce
horror in a beholder.

machination—a scheming or crafty
action or artful design intended
to accomplish some usually
evil end.

magic—manipulation of the
unseen forces of nature
(usually for selfish ends)—
white magic is said to be the
right or ethical use of spiritual
power; SORCERY, WIZARD-
RY, WITCHCRAFT.

Mammon—material wealth or
possessions, especially as
having a debasing influence.

mantle—a symbol of preeminence
or authority.

mantra—a Vedic hymn or prayer;
a verbal spell, ritualistic
incantation, or mystic formula
used devotionally and as an
object of meditation in
Hinduism, Jainism, Buddhism,
etc.; a power phrase or mystic
sound, syllables composed of
vowels and consonants used
for focusing the mind.

marauding—roaming about and
raiding in search of plunder.

Masters—supernormal agents
believed to reside in the
Himalayan heights or other
inaccessible realms; belief in
is based on view that there are
latent possibilities in the
human body and mind which,
when developed through
appropriate disciplines, can
place at the command of an
adept unseen, intelligent forces
of nature which enable him to
perform extraordinary feats

beyond the capacity of normal men; one who inspires devotion or reverence on the part of his disciples; a religious or enlightened teacher whose guidance is sought after.

meditation—a natural psychosomatic exercise involving attention or concentration of mind as the instrument by which nature accelerates the process of evolution; with cultivation of noble traits of character and self-mastery, the method prescribed in all religious systems and occult doctrines for gaining to higher states of consciousness or to God.

mediumship—a highly erratic and unpredictable phenomenon in which an individual is held to act as a channel of communication between the earthly world and a world of spirits; many mediumistic communications are nothing but expressions of the subconscious; AUTOMATISM.

meet (adj.)—precisely adapted to a particular situation, need, or circumstance: very proper; FIT.

millennial—of or relating to a millenium (a period of 1000 years); ages long.

Monod, Jacques (1910–1976)— French molecular biologist who collaborated with Francois Jacob in developing the concepts of messenger RNA (ribonucleic acid) and the operon. For this work, Monod and Jacob shared the 1965 Nobel Prize for physiology and medicine with another French biologist. In his biological and philosophical work *Le Hasard et la Necessite* (1971; *Chance and Necessity),* Monod draws upon recent biochemical discoveries to contend that all forms of life result from random mutation (chance) and Darwinian selection (necessity). He concludes that there is no master plan of creation or pre-existing purpose in life and that man must choose his own values in a vast and otherwise indifferent universe.

morass—something that traps, confuses, or impedes.

Mullah—a learned teacher or expounder of the religious law and doctrines of Islam.

mystic—one who has attained to the next step on the ladder of human evolution and has knowledge from a superphysical source; one with a more evolved human brain in tune with the spiritual realities of the universe, able to gather knowledge not available to the intellect alone, and receptive to Revelation; a superman, a prophet, Buddha, Christ, Mohammed, Quetzalcoatl, Moses, Krishna; a savior, an adept, a yogi, an initiate, an illumined sage, an enlightened seer; see MYSTICAL EXPERIENCE.

mystical experience—the target of human evolution and a more evolved form of consciousness; although known as union with God, it is still far from the consciousness of God or the Absolute; the whole spiritual, esoteric, occult, hermetic, and alchemic literature of mankind revolves around this potentiality in the human brain; the source of all human concepts of Divinity and Transcendental Realities.

mystic vision—the union of the Soul with the Over-Soul or the individual self with Universal Consciousness; the supreme experience which reveals the majesty, infinite awareness, and immortal nature of the soul; a transhuman state of consciousness receptive to Revelation; the "vision of God" and the basis of religions; see MYSTICAL EXPERIENCE.

narcosis—a state of stupor, unconsciousness, or arrested activity produced by the influence of narcotics or other chemicals.

nefarious—flagrantly wicked or impious: EVIL; VICIOUS.

Nemesis—the Greek goddess of fate and punisher of extravagant pride.

nescient—lacking knowledge or awareness: IGNORANT.

Nirvana—(Hinduism, Jainism, Buddhism): the state of freedom from karma, extinction of desire, passion, illusion, and the ego, and the attainment of serenity, truth, and unchanging

being: SALVATION, MYSTICAL EXPERIENCE; commonly treated as "extinction" or "annihilation," but is in actual fact the effacement of the dividing line between the individual and the Cosmic Consciousness.

occult (n.)—matters regarded as involving the action or influence of superphysical agencies or some secret knowledge of them.

occultism—occult theory or practice: a belief in supernormal agents and in hidden or mysterious powers and the possibility of subjecting them to human control; stripped of superstition (the literal interpretation of symbols) and exaggerated claims, occult systems describe the evolution of consciousness.

Om—or Aum: the most important sacred sound in the Vedic and Hindu traditions, used as a symbol and expression of Brahman, and as an object of meditation (placed at the beginning of works, like "Hail," and at the end, like "Amen"); the music of the soul witnessed and apprehended by saints, mystics, and yogis.

orbs—EYES; spherical bodies, especially celestial spheres.

palsied—affected with paralysis or uncontrollable tremors of the body or a part.

pander—to act as a pander (someone who caters to or exploits

the weaknesses of others);
especially, to provide gratifi-
tion for others' desires.

patrician—aristocratic.

patron—one who uses his wealth
or influence to help an individual, an institution, or a
cause.

perfidious—faithless or disloyal;
UNRELIABLE; violating alle-
giance: TREACHEROUS.

pernicious—highly injurious or
destructive: DEADLY; BANE-
FUL, NOXIOUS.

phobic—having an aversion for;
motivated by or based on with-
drawal from an unpleasant
stimulus rather than movement
toward a pleasant one.

plumb—to measure the depth of.

portentous—prophetic; ominous.

potentate—one who wields controlling power.

precept—a command or principle
intended as a general rule of
action; an order issued by
legally constituted authority
to a subordinate.

precipice—a very steep or overhanging place; the brink of
disaster.

precocious—exceptionally early in
development or occurrence.

prediluvian—pre-deluge.

prevarication—deviation from the
truth: LIE.

primordial—existing in or persist-
ing from the beginning:
PRIMEVAL; FUNDAMEN-
TAL, PRIMARY.

probity—adherence to the highest
principles and ideals:
UPRIGHTNESS; HONESTY.

profusion—lavish expenditure:
EXTRAVAGANCE.

prophet—one who speaks for God
or a deity: a divinely inspired
revealer, interpreter, or spokes-
person; one gifted with more
than ordinary spiritual and
moral insight; from the Greek,
prophetes: one who "tells
forth" a divinely inspired
message and who "foretells"
the future; all revelation, i.e.,
knowledge deemed to come
from a superphysical source,
is prophecy (see REVELA-
TION); SEER, MYSTIC.

propitiate—to gain or regain the
favor or goodwill of: AP-
PEASE, CONCILIATE.

prosaic—DULL, UNIMAGINA-
TIVE; belonging to or suitable
for the everyday world; having
a plain practical unimaginative
quality or character.

psychic (n.)—a person apparently
sensitive to superphysical
forces and influences.

pugnacious—having a belligerent
nature; CRUEL, SAVAGE;
DEADLY, DESTRUCTIVE.

rank (adj.)—luxuriantly or exces-
sively vigorous in growth;
shockingly conspicuous; EX-
CESSIVE; offensively gross
or coarse: FOUL.

redemption—FULFILLMENT,
spiritual salvation, rebirth.

redoubtable—FORMIDABLE;
ILLUSTRIOUS.

remission—release, relief; MOD-
ERATION; POSTPONE-
MENT; DEFERMENT,
ABATEMENT.

Revelation—an act of revealing or communicating divine truth, especially God's disclosure or manifestation of himself or of his will to man; knowledge deemed to come from a super-physical source; that which provides the sole authority for human concepts about Trans-cendental Realities; see PROPHET.

ribald—CRUDE, OFFENSIVE.

sacrosanct—most sacred or holy.

sadhu—a (usually) Hindu mendi-cant ascetic, often claiming great mystic powers, wearing a saffron robe or abjuring all clothing, and often practicing extreme mortification.

Sahaja—(Sanskrit term for "born together"): the unitive state of perception (a state of mystical union with Divinity) and the perennial state of ecstasy (supreme beatitude) which become a normal possession of the enlightened person; used in Sikh and Indian mystical writ-ings; MYSTICAL EXPERI-ENCE.

saint—one eminent for devoutness or virtue; one officially re-cognized, especially through canonization, as preeminent for purity and transcendence; a holy or godly person, one spiritually reborn or under-going spiritual rebirth; see MYSTIC.

salve (v.)—QUIET, ASSUAGE.

Samadhi—(Hinduism, Buddhism, Jainism): a state of deep con-centration resulting in ecstatic or rapt contemplation of the inner reality of consciousness; union with or absorption into ultimate reality; the summit of Patanjali's Eight Limbs of Yoga, the final step of Buddha's Eightfold Path; spiritual self-fulfillment, ENLIGHTENMENT, MYSTI-CAL EXPERIENCE.

sans—WITHOUT.

sapient—possessing or expressing great sagacity or discernment; WISE.

Satori—sudden enlightenment, a state of consciousness attained by intuitive illumination repre-senting the spiritual goal of Zen Buddhism; MYSTICAL EXPERIENCE.

savant—a man of learning, espe-cially a person with detailed knowledge in some specialized field.

schism—DIVISION, SEPARATION; DISCORD, DISHARMONY.

scourge—WHIP, especially one used to inflict pain or punishment.

self-immolation—a deliberate and willing sacrifice of oneself; self-destruction.

sentient—responsive to or con-scious of sense impressions; AWARE; finely sensitive in perception or feeling.

sentinel—a soldier standing guard at a point of passage (as a gate).

sepulchres—places of burial: TOMBS.

seraphs—the six-winged angels standing in the presence of

God; an order of angels.

Serpent-Power—regenerative energy universally symbolized by a serpent and worshipped as the Mother Goddess, Female Principle of Energy, or Virgin of Wisdom (Isis, Shakti, Earth Mother, Virgin Mary, Sophia); also known as *parakletos* (from the New Testament) and *speirema* (from the Greek, meaning the serpent-coil, or serpent force); in the Vedas, addressed as *Vak,* goddess of speech; in Egyptian, *messi* (messiah) is the name of a serpent designated the "Sacred Word" *(Logos);* as the Hieroglyphic *Tet* sign, the serpent also means speech, language, to declare (Revelation); also known as *Kundalini* (from Sanskrit), meaning "coiled up" like a slumbering snake or a coiled spring, implying latent power or untapped potential, traditionally symbolized in Hindu texts as a sleeping serpent coiled at the base of the human spine, indicating its close connection with the reproductive organs and life force; has been described in the ancient records of Tibet, Egypt, Sumer, China, Greece, and other cultures and traditions.

sheaves (n.)—quantities of the stalks and ears of a cereal grass or sometimes other plant material bound together.

shibboleths—CATCHWORDS,

SLOGANS; words or phrases used to express a characteristic position or stand or goal to be achieved.

siddhis—psychical powers of the type mentioned by Patanjali in his Yoga-Sutras (circa 4th century B.C. to 4th century A.D.); miraculous power or supernatural talents which legendary Yogis are said to have exercised; Yogic attainments, a by-product of success in Yoga.

sidereal—of, relating to, or expressed in relation to stars or constellations: ASTRAL.

signal (adj.)—distinguished from the ordinary; NOTICEABLE.

solacious—alleviating grief or anxiety; cheerful, soothing.

sorcery—an endeavor to control or bend the powers of the world to man's will: MAGIC, WIZARDRY, WITCHCRAFT.

spur (n.)—a ridge or lesser elevation that extends laterally from a mountain or mountain range.

specter—something that haunts or perturbs the mind: PHANTASM.

specious—having deceptive attraction or allure; having a false look of truth or genuineness; plausible but fallacious.

sprite—a disembodied spirit: GHOST.

stalwarts—unwavering partisans.

summum bonum—the supreme good from which all others are derived.

superstition—a belief, conception, act, or practice resulting from ignorance, unreasoning fear, trust in magic, or a false conception of causation; irrational dogma; the root of such beliefs is in taking a symbol for a literal fact.

surrogate—something that serves as a substitute.

Tantra—(from the Sanskrit, *tan,* to believe, to have faith in; hence, literally, an instrument or means of faith): Hindu and Buddhist systems based on extensive sacred compositions assuming the form of a dialogue between the God Shiva, Male Principle of Wisdom, and his bride, the Goddess Shakti, Female Principle of Energy; the goal of this religious system is the integration of these two principles in man, represented by the union of Shiva and Shakti.

tantrik—a follower of the mystical system of the Tantra; a scholar, a philosopher, a yogi; tellurian earthly. See TANTRA.

tithe (n.)—TENTH; broadly: a small part.

torpor—a state of mental and motor inactivity with partial or total insensibility: extreme sluggishness or stagnation of function; APATHY, DULLNESS.

trammels—things impeding activity, progress, or freedom: RESTRAINTS.

transcendent—beyond what is perceived or presented in sensory experience: DIVINE, MYSTICAL, SUPER-PHYSICAL.

transgressions—infringements or violations of a law, command, or duty.

trenchant—KEEN, SHARP; CAUSTIC; INCISIVE.

twaddle—silly idle talk: DRIVEL; NONSENSE.

umbrageous—SHADY.

unfathomable—not capable of being fathomed (penetrated and come to be understood); impossible to comprehend; IMMEASURABLE.

U.N.O.—United Nations Organization.

urbanity—smooth although superficial affability and politeness.

vagaries—erratic, unpredictable, or extravagant manifestations, actions, or notions; WHIMS, CAPRICES.

vagarious—erratic, unpredictable, or extravagant; CAPRICIOUS, WHIMSICAL.

vagrant (adj.)—having a fleeting, wayward, or inconstant quality; having no fixed course: RANDOM.

vassal—a person under the protection of another who is his (feudal) lord and to whom he has vowed homage and fealty; one in a subservient or subordinate position.

verdant—unripe in experience or judgement: GREEN.

vermin—small common harmful or objectionable animals that are difficult to control.

vindication—CONFIRMATION, SUBSTANTIATION; DE-

FENSE, JUSTIFICATION.

viz.—namely.

voluptuaries—those for whom the chief interest is luxury and the gratification of sensual appetites.

vortex—a magnetic or impelling force by which something may be engulfed; a current running contrary to the main current.

vouchsafe—to grant or furnish often in a gracious or condescending manner; to give by way of reply; to grant as a privilege or special favor; GRANT.

wantonness—unrestrained extravagance; capriciousness, recklessness.

weal—a sound, healthy, or prosperous state: WELL-BEING.

Wilberforce, Samuel, Bishop of Oxford (19th century)—In 1861, at a meeting in Oxford of the British Association for the Advancement of Science, the Bishop attacked the concept of Darwinian Evolution and brought down upon the Christian Church the bitterness of Thomas H. Huxley and his followers.

wizard—SORCERER, MAGICIAN.

worthies—prominent persons.

Yoga—(derived from the Sanskrit root *yug,* which means "to yoke," "join," or "union"): signifies both the object attained, namely, union of the Soul and the Over-Soul, and also the method or methods by which this union is achieved; aim of is to accelerate the process of evolution, a natural process already at work in the human organism, to open new areas of supersensory perception in the brain capable of manifesting a transhuman state of consciousness receptive to Revelation; any and all spiritual disciplines that aim at attaining oneness with the Supreme Intelligence; the main exercise of these disciplines, in addition to moral and ethical self-development, is fixity of attention, i.e., meditation or systematized concentration using symbols corresponding to the faith or belief of the aspirant.

yogi—one in possession of an activated supersensory organ of perception able to gather knowledge not available to the intellect alone and receptive to Revelation; one who has attained union with higher consciousness, i.e, Brahman, God, Kingdom of Heaven, Nirvana, Allah, Cosmic Consciousness; YOGA-ADEPT, ENLIGHTENED, SEER, MYSTIC, INITIATE.

Zen—a Japanese school of Mahayana Buddhism that teaches self-discipline, deep meditation, and the attainment of enlightenment by direct intuitive insight into a self-validating transcendent truth beyond all intellectual conceptions, and typically expresses its teachings in paradoxical and nonlogical forms.